THE
Duct
Tape
Book

25 PROJECTS TO MAKE
WITH DUCT TAPE

Jolie Dobson

FIREFLY BOOKS

A FIREFLY BOOK

Published by Firefly Books Ltd. 2012

Second printing

Publisher Cataloging-in-Publication Data (U.S.)
Dobson, Jolie.
  The duct tape book : 25 projects to make
with duct tape / Jolie Dobson.
[144] p. : col. photos. ; cm.
ISBN-13: 978-1-77085-098-9 (pbk.)
1. Duct tape. 2. Handicraft. I. Title.
745.5 dc23   TT880.D6376 2012

Library and Archives Canada Cataloguing in Publication
Dobson, Jolie, 1981-
  The duct tape book : 25 projects to make with duct tape
/ Jolie Dobson.
ISBN 978-1-77085-098-9
1. Handicraft. 2. Duct tape. I. Title. II. Title: Twenty-five
projects to make with duct tape.
TT880.D52 2012   745.5   C2012-902990-4

Published in the United States by
Firefly Books (U.S.) Inc.
P.O. Box 1338, Ellicott Station
Buffalo, New York 14205

Published in Canada by
Firefly Books Ltd.
50 Staples Avenue, Unit 1,
Richmond Hill, Ontario L4B 0A7

Cover and interior design: Jacqueline Hope Raynor.
Cover model: Jolie Dobson. Interior model: Allison Worek.

Printed in China

The publisher gratefully acknowledges the financial support for our
publishing program by the Government of Canada through the Canada
Book Fund as administered by the Department of Canadian Heritage.

Contents

Introduction

Projects

Introduction

Duct tape was called "the handyman's secret weapon" by Red Green. It's been stowed on board every space flight since the Gemini missions in the mid-1960s. And dollars to donuts it's holding something together right now in your house, car or garage. But the biggest secret about the magic fix-all tape is that it is the ultimate craft material too! Its tensile strength lends itself well to sturdy construction, its resistance to water means it's suitable for outdoor use and now that it comes in colors other than silver it offers a vivid palette for artists, fashion designers and craftspeople in their creations and projects.

In fact, duct tape DIY has become a cultural phenomenon — the Internet has exploded with duct tape art sites, forums and blogs. Indeed, the 25 projects that follow in these pages are a testament to the tape's versatility and style and are shown in step-by-step fashion so you too, armed with a few rolls, tools and some basic rip and fold moves, can master the sticky stuff and become a duct tape *sensei*!

Duct Tape History

Duct tape was invented for the U.S. military by the cool-sounding Revolite Corporation (then a division of Johnson & Johnson) in 1942. Originally designed to seal ammunition cases, the tape was tough, durable and fantastically water-resistant and was promptly enlisted to repair anything that was broken, including jeeps, firearms and aircraft.

Because the adhesive tape had a canvas (or duck cloth) backing and repelled water like certain feathered fowl, it was quickly dubbed "duck" tape by WWII soldiers. Somewhere along the way (where exactly is a hotly debated topic amongst duct tape historians) there was a gloss from "duck" to "duct" tape. This is odd as the tape is rarely used on ducts — in fact many building codes forbid it for this use! Now Duck®Tape is a brand of duct tape.

The utilitarian effectiveness of duct tape meant the humble gun-metal silver roll would find its way into toolkits in practically every profession and home around the world, and today it is known as "gaffer tape," "racer tape," "riggers' tape" or "100-mph tape" (it was used to balance helicopter blades in the Vietnam War), and is regularly used where something absolutely positively needs to be taped down for good.

Duct tape was famously used to repair the CO_2 scrubbers on the lunar module of *Apollo 13*, providing much-needed oxygen to that mission's marooned astronauts, and more recently, a few carefully placed silver slivers proved to be a low-tech but very effective fix for the Apple iPhone 4's flaky antenna.

Duct tape's explosive popularity grows as people explore its creative possibilities for fun instead of just its practical uses. Everything from prom dresses to artistic shoe repair can be made by this magic tape. In this book, learn to craft everything from a handy bike pannier to bodacious bow ties, from a decorated smartphone case to a customizable purse! Join the fun and master the sticky stuff to be a part of one of the most exciting and creative trends of the decade!

Getting Started

Tools you will need:

- Craft knife
- Scissors
- Ruler
- Large cutting board
- Sewing tape measure
- Compass

Useful material for your duct tape projects:

Snaps: Snaps are a sturdy way of holding things together and can give your project a polished look. They can, however, be difficult to position and attach.

Velcro: Hook-and-loop fasteners such as Velcro can be used where clasps are required, such as clothing or a lunch bag. While easy to apply if using the self-adhesive variety, they do not hold as well as snaps. You might want to consider sewing pieces of Velcro onto some projects for added security.

Zippers: Depending on the shape of your project, attaching zippers can be fairly easy, though figuring out the measurements can be a bit tricky. Zippers can hold with just duct tape, but to be safe it's best to sew the zipper on as well, then cover the stitches with tape.

Twist ties: Used for decorations, such as the tail on a piggy bank (see page 97).

Shredded newspaper and plastic produce bags: Used to create round shapes for animal projects such as a rabbit (see page 125).

Coat hangers: Used for support in projects such as a basket (see page 129).

Choosing Tape

Because it is not trademarked, there are many varieties of duct tape on the market, so buyer beware — not all brands are the real thing! Always look for cloth-backed adhesive tape. Accept no substitutes.

Thinner duct tape is better suited to making clothing or other projects that require flexibility. Thicker duct tape (sometimes called "professional grade" or "industrial grade") has more cloth fibers for increased strength and tends to be more expensive, but is better for projects that require more rigidity.

Of course, standard-issue silver or gray duct tape is cheaper than the colored stuff and comes in bigger rolls. If you can't find colored duct tape at your local craft or hardware stores, you can certainly order them online.

Credits for duct tape used in book

The patterns of duct tape running along the sides of the projects in this book are from the following companies, and can be purchased through their websites.

Duck® Tape appears on the sides of the following pages: 14-37, 42-51, 70-75, 114-123, 128-133, 138-144. Duck®, and Duck® Tape are registered trademarks of ShurTech Brands, LLC, used with permission. Visit www.duckbrand.com to view all of the available patterns and browse the online store.

Platypus® Designer Duct Tape™ appears on sides of the following pages: 3-13, 38-41, 52-69, 76-113, 102-113, 124-127, 134-137. Visit www.designerducttape.com to view new and current patterns and to buy online.

Colors and Customizing Projects

With a rainbow of duct tape colors now available, try casting your project in a new color: chrome, electric blue, neon pink or prints like tie-dye, polka dot, zebra skin or camouflage! Use your imagination. Put rolls of different colored duct tape side by side to see if you like them together. Choosing complementary colors on the color wheel (say, blue and orange) for contrast can create vibrant results. Change up a project by switching colors and decorations. Create a zoo of animals from a single project by picking different colors and altering facial features like ears, nose and eyes. Remember, there are no wrong colors!

Stencils and Decorating

You can decorate your projects with any shape or design, simple or intricate. But remember, the more detailed the design, the more precision and patience you will need! Stencils can make tracing out your design easier.

First, draw your design onto a piece of poster board or card stock and cut it out. Place a piece of tape sticky-side down on your cutting board. (For bigger designs, line up and stick together a few pieces of tape to form a sheet sticky-side down.) Tape your stencil onto the piece of tape or sheet using smaller loops of tape. Carefully trace around your stencil with a craft knife, making sure you cut through the fibers in the tape so that it peels off the cutting board perfectly when you are finished.

And last, don't throw out your cut-offs! Save these little scraps of tape from the garbage and use them to add tassels, fringe, hair or other decorations and details to your projects. You'll never know when they'll come in handy.

What are you waiting for? Reach for the roll and start taping!

How to Make Duct Tape Sheets

The basic building block of many of a duct tape project, these sheets are built up from strips of folded, overlapping tape. It's a good idea to make your strips of tape longer than the width you need (by at least 1"), and trim your sheet down to size afterwards. This will give you clean edges and square right angles. You also won't have to measure each piece of tape — just measure the first piece and use that as your guide for the rest. You may want to seal cut edges of the sheet with a folded over piece of tape to get a finished, non-sticky edge.

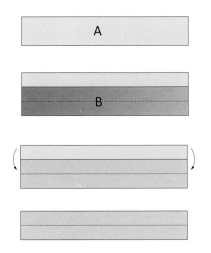

1 On a cutting board, cut a piece of duct tape to the width you need and place it sticky side up (A).

2 Cut a second piece of tape (B) the same length as the first and place it sticky side down, halfway down piece A.

3 Fold the sticky half of piece A down on the non-sticky side of piece B. This is your first sealed edge.

4 Flip the pieces of tape over and place a third piece of tape (C) over the sticky part of piece B.

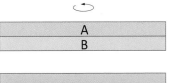

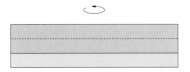

5 Flip again and repeat as necessary for the length of sheet you need.

6 After adding your last piece of tape, fold over the last exposed sticky side to seal the final edge.

How to Make Duct Tape Straps

Straps are used for belts, loops, handles and other means of securing your projects. Whether it's for a knapsack, lunch bag or bike pannier, straps can be made thicker for greater rigidity. Depending on the strength required, you may need to use snaps or Velcro to fasten your straps.

1 Take a piece of duct tape the length you need and fold it in half horizontally. This will give you about a 1" strap. If you need a wider strap, fold the top and bottom edges of the tape in towards the center, leaving an exposed sticky strip in the middle of the tape. This is piece A.

A

1"

Alternate method for wider strap widths

2 Take a second piece of tape (B) the same length as the first and place it sticky side up. Place piece A in the center of piece B. If you made your strap wider than 1" and have an exposed sticky strip across the middle of piece A, place the sticky side down on piece B.

3 Fold the sticky edges of piece B over piece A.

4 You should now have one clean, smooth side on your strap, which will be the front face.

5 Attach snaps or Velcro if needed, following the directions provided with them.

Taping Flat Surfaces

Taping flat surfaces will be a common step in many duct tape projects. This method is also great for making large sheets. Having trouble controlling and lining up long pieces of tape for those super-sized sheets? No problem! Just tape smaller sheets of duct tape together to create a bigger one. If you accidentally cut your duct tape sheet too small, you can extend the sheet by this method too.

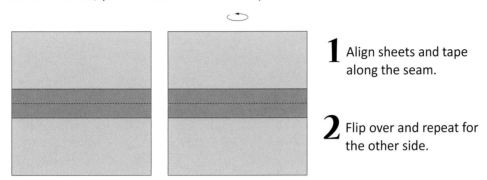

1 Align sheets and tape along the seam.

2 Flip over and repeat for the other side.

Taping Right-Angle Flat Surfaces

For sheets that meet at a right angle, it's best to tape the seam when the two sheets are lying flat (see "Taping Flat Surfaces" above) then fold into a right angle. If this is not possible (for example the final corner of a box), tape the inside seam first, where you won't see the tape. With the corner secured, you can then tape the outside corner, and get a cleaner result.

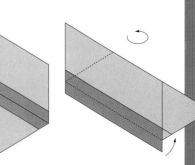

1 When taping an inside right-angled seam, make sure you push the piece of tape as far into the corner as possible.

2 On an outside right-angled corner, place and smooth out the piece of tape on one side of the corner first and then fold over.

11

Taping Curved Edges

To tape curved edges you can use a series of different sizes and shapes of tape: rectangles, squares, triangles or diamonds. Different shapes and sizes make it easier to tape around a curve without getting ripples in the tape or edges that stick up.

1 Cut out the small pieces of tape in a shape that works best with your project.

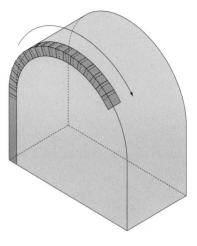

2 Overlap the pieces as you tape around the curve. If the edge sticks up at the fold of the tape you can cut it and stick it flat. Make sure to overlap your next piece of tape on top of the cut to hide it and make it secure.

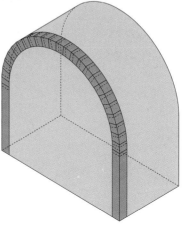

Taping Curved Surfaces

There are two ways to tape a curved surface with duct tape:

1 Cover the surface with overlapping ellipse- or almond-shaped pieces of tape like a beach ball. While much neater, this method requires more precise measurements. Cap the top and bottom where all points meet with a circular piece of tape.

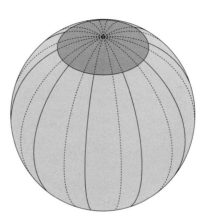

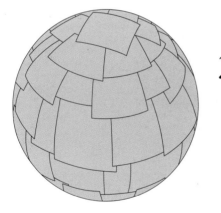

2 Apply a patchwork of tape around the curved surface. You can use square, rectangular, or circular pieces of tape. Overlap the pieces and place them in a way to avoid wrinkling. If wrinkling occurs, carefully use a craft knife to slice the wrinkle in the middle and overlap another piece of tape on top. While easier than the first method, the results do not look as neat.

bike buddy

a riff on the old-fashioned canvas or leather saddle-bag slung in pairs over a horse, J.B. Wood's 1884 bicycle pannier (U.S. Patent No. 299609) is used today to ferry around all manner of modern things, such as work clothes, courier packages, bike locks, laptops, camping gear and groceries (the term does come from the Old French for "bread," after all). This smart, two-tone duct tape version is custom-fit to your bike rack, and because it's made of the tape, it will stand up to the elements and keep your cargo dry. Sling this over your beast of burden and pedal in style.

What You'll Need

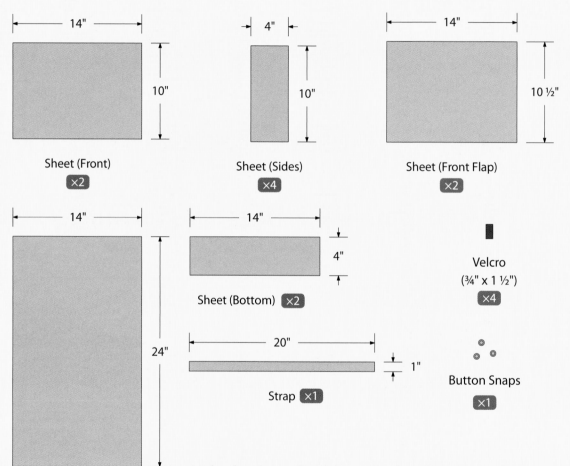

14"

10"

Sheet (Front)
×2

4"

10"

Sheet (Sides)
×4

14"

10 ½"

Sheet (Front Flap)
×2

14"

24"

Back
×1

14"

4"

Sheet (Bottom) ×2

20"

1"

Strap ×1

Velcro
(¾" x 1 ½")
×4

Button Snaps
×1

Make the sheets for the pannier (see "How to Make Duct Tape Sheets" on page 8). Measure your bike rack first to ensure it fits and adjust the measurements as needed. Use contrasting colors of tape for the front flap and back sheets for a snazzier look.

1 Place one of the front sheets in the middle and tape two side sheets and a bottom sheet to it along the three edges as shown, taping the seams on both sides (see "Taping Flat Surfaces" on page 11).

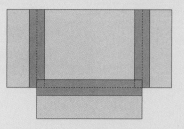

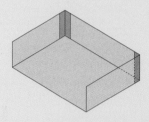

2 Fold up the bottom and side sheets and tape the two corners where the sides and bottom meet, creating a three-sided box. Tape the seams inside and out (see "Taping Right-Angle Flat Surfaces" on page 11). Repeat Steps 1 and 2 to make a second three-sided box for the other side of the pannier.

3 Take the large back sheet and mark the middle of the two longest sides. You will need to cut two 1" slots in the middle of the back sheet, but the design and style of your bike rack will determine where you need to cut the slots. These slots will be used to feed the strap through to hold your pannier onto your bike rack. (In this example, the bike rack has cross bars 3" from each end of the rack.) Cut a 1" wide strap to the required length and add snaps to each end of the strap, following the instructions provided with the snaps.

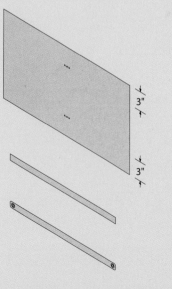

3"

3"

17

4 Take the first three-sided box from Step 2 and place it at one end of the back sheet, with the open end of the box facing the middle. Secure the bottom and sides of the box to the back sheet, taping seams both inside and out (see "Taping Right-Angle Flat Surfaces" on page 11). Repeat with the other three-sided box.

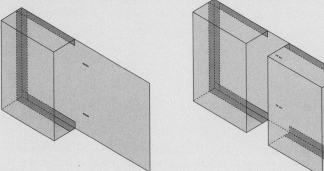

5 Take one of the front flap sheets and tape it to the back sheet, aligning it with the top opening of the box and taping the seams on both sides. Rotate and repeat with the other front flap.

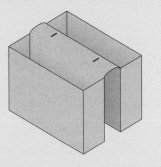 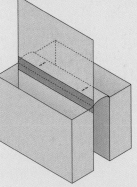

6 Make four tabs by folding 2" x 3" pieces of tape in half so they measure 2" x 1 ½".

×4

7 Tape the tabs 2 ½" in from either side on the back of the front flaps, leaving ½" overhang. Run a piece of tape along the bottom of the front flap on the outside, completely covering the tabs and about ¼" of the front flap. Carefully cut this piece of tape down the sides of each tab and fold it over onto the back of the front flap. Repeat for the other side of the pannier.

8 Add self-adhesive Velcro to the underside of the tabs and the front of the pannier.

9 To secure the pannier to your bike rack, feed the strap through one of the slots, under and around the rack and up through the other slot. Snap the strap closed.

19

funky frame bag

Lock, cell phone, keys, wallet. No, it's not a memory aid to help you remember your license plate, it's a list of things cyclists slap themselves on the head over after they've fallen out of their pockets. Whether you're training for a long tour or just commuting to work or school, this cute, durable rear frame bag will keep these cycling essentials safe. Slim and compact, it loops over your bike's top frame and snaps around the down tube beneath the seat, and won't interfere with rider movement. Use brightly colored duct tape and it can double as a reflector! Snaps are better than self-adhesive Velcro to ensure strength, however sewing in patches of Velcro will do the job just as well.

What You'll Need

Button Snaps
×3

Strap
×1

6 ½"

¾"

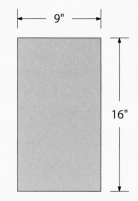

9"

16"

Sheet
×1

Make the sheet and strap (see "How to Make Duct Tape Sheets" on page 8 and "How to Make Duct Tape Straps" on page 10). Carefully measure your bike frame first, adjusting the measurements of the sheet and strap to accommodate the circumference of the frame, brake wires and other things that may get in the way.

1 Fold the sheet 5 ½" up from the bottom and 3 ¼" down from the top.

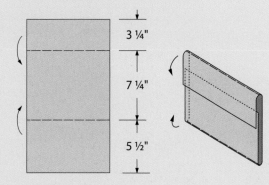

3 ¼"

7 ¼"

5 ½"

2 Add snaps ¾" in from the top and bottom edges and 1 ¾" in from either side. Follow the directions provided with the snaps, ensuring the snaps are facing the right way.

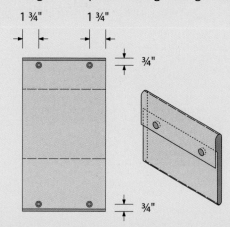

1 ¾"   1 ¾"

¾"

¾"

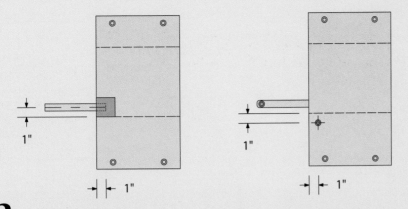

3 Tape the strap to the sheet with its width centered 1" above the bottom fold, and 1" in from the left edge. To place the snaps, mark a point on the sheet 1" in from the left edge and 1" below the bottom fold and make a small hole. Fold up the bottom of the sheet to ensure the free end of the strap is aligned with the hole. Round the free end of the strap into a semi-circle and hammer in the snaps to the sheet and strap according to the directions provided with the snaps.

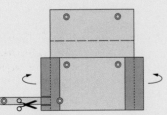

4 Fold the bottom of the sheet up and tape the sides inside and out. On the side with the strap, carefully cut down the sides of the strap before folding the tape around.

5 Decorate!

fab frames

the art of the tape need not be limited to 100 percent duct tape creations. Indeed, a new "coat" of tape can give new life to a cast-off object or a flea market find. Take picture frames — how many times have you searched in vain for just the right frame to match the still life you want to hang on the dining room wall? Well, take an old frame and jazz it up with patterns or give it more depth by adding duct tape leaves or other shapes. These are but a few examples — let your imagination run free and personalize your own window on the world.

What You'll Need

The following instructions are for the single leaf bunch (large). The same process applies for the small leaf and yellow flower bunches.

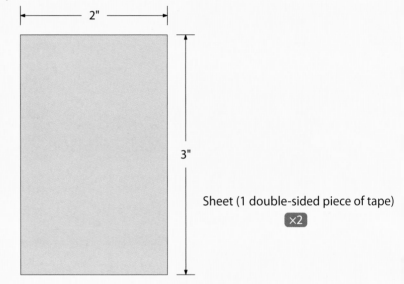

Sheet (1 double-sided piece of tape)

×2

1 For the garden frame, cover the picture frame in duct tape.

2 To make leaves, cut a double-sided piece of duct tape the length you want your leaves to be by taping two pieces together, sticky sides facing each other.

3 Cut out a leaf shape.

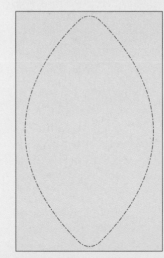

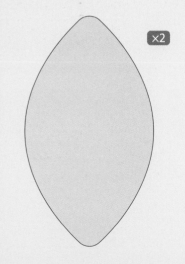

×2

4 Pinch one end of the leaf together and wrap with a small piece of duct tape to curve the edges of the leaf upward and make it three-dimensional. Repeat for the second leaf.

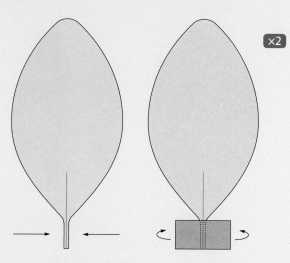

5 Take the two leaves and wrap tape around the two pinched ends to secure them together.

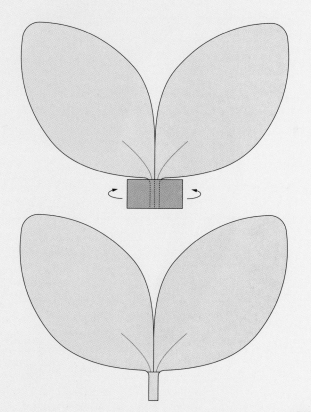

6 Repeat with different sizes and colors of tape and stick the leaves around the frame.

hot pink handbag

the handbag was created when Samuel Parkinson, a British confectioner during the mid 1800s and the man behind butterscotch, had various larger bags custom made for his wife to ride the railways in style, because let's face it, those tiny coin purses just didn't cut it for the modern woman. (Don't listen to those who say Otzi the Iceman got there first more than 5,000 years ago with his "man purse" full of arrows. And if you think we're making this up, there's a handbag museum in Amsterdam, too.) Today there is a dizzying array of handbags — hobos, clutches, saddles, baguettes, bucket bags — made from denim, leather, canvas, nylon and faux fur, so why not duct tape? This stylish hot pink model can be modified by lengthening the handles.

What You'll Need

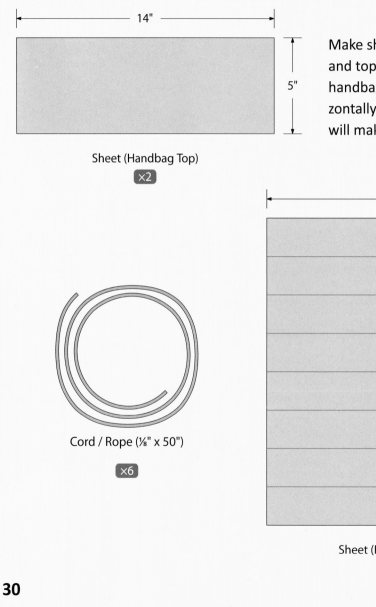

14"

5"

Sheet (Handbag Top)
×2

Make sheets for the handbag body and top. For the main body of the handbag, run the duct tape horizontally (across the width). This will make the pleats fold better.

Cord / Rope (⅛" x 50")
×6

14"

16"

Sheet (Handbag Main)
×1

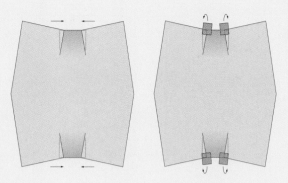

1 On the top and bottom of the main sheet, make four marks 5" and 6" in from each side. Take the 5" mark and fold in onto the 6" mark, making a pleat. Try to keep the fold as parallel to the top of the sheet as possible. Repeat for all four pleats. Fold a small piece of tape over the edges of the sheet to secure them in place.

2 Take one of the two top sheets for the handbag and center it widthwise along the top edge of the main sheet with the pleats. Tape the top sheet along its width about ½" down over the pleats of the handbag or until the top edge of the pleats is covered. Fold the top sheet in half horizontally to the reverse side of the handbag and tape again. Repeat with the second top sheet at the bottom. (You may want to cut the tape a little bit at the pleats so that the tape lays flat.) The folded top sheets will be longer than the main part of the handbag. Trim the excess vertically to the point where the folded-over sheets intersect with the main sheet. The folded top sheets will create channels for the handbag handles to go through.

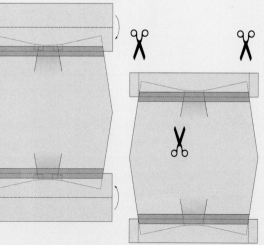

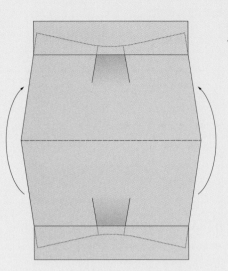

3 Make a soft fold in the middle of the handbag, bringing the two top folded sheets together. Tape the sides of the handbag together, starting at the bottom edge of the folded top sheets and ending 1" from the bottom of the handbag.

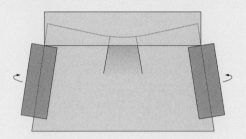

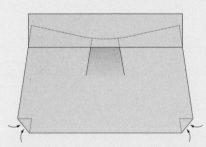

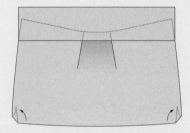

4 Both sides of the handbag will now have a 1" hole at the bottom. Push the corner of the handbag through the hole to the inside of the handbag at a 45° angle. On the inside, pull this fold back towards the side of the bag and tape to hold in place. Repeat for the other side. Tape the sides of the handbag on the inside as well.

5 For the handles of the handbag, cover six 50" lengths of thin rope in duct tape. Take three pieces of rope for each handle of the handbag and braid together. Alternatively, make two straps out of duct tape or just cover two pieces of rope. The length of the handles can vary depending on what kind of purse you want.

6 Run each handle through the channel created in the top sheets in Step 2 and tape the ends of the braid together by wrapping with duct tape. Hide the taped ends of the handle in the channel. After both handles are in place, tape up the remaining sides of the handbag.

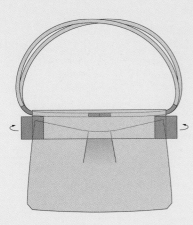

smart phone holder

human beings just can't help accessorizing a new purchase, and wireless devices like cell phones are no exception. Indeed, after springing for the latest iPhone, Blackberry or Droid, a cell phone case is *de rigeur* (that's French for gotta have it) to stow your phone between tweeting, surfing and streaming. But why cover that hot new smart phone with a silly piece of expensive plastic when you can create this unique handcrafted holder from the finest duct tape for just pennies? This simple-to-make, rugged cell phone holster can be easily customized (use offcuts of different colored duct tape to make stripes, patterns or designs — your imagination is the limit!), and because you make it, it will fit *any* phone.

What You'll Need

3"

5 ¼"

Front / Back

Make two sheets for the front and back of the case (see "How to Make Duct Tape Sheets" on page 8). Measure your cell phone first to ensure a good fit, adding about ¼" on either side to accommodate its width.

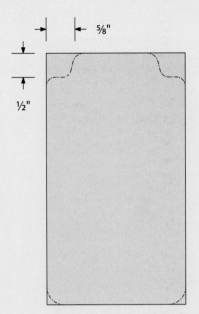

5/8"

1/2"

1 Mark two squares at the top corners, 5/8" in from both sides and 1/2" down from the top.

2 Holding the two sheets together with paper clips or tape, cut out the squares and carefully round the corners. Round the bottom corners as well. You now have two identically shaped sheets for either side of the case.

3 Cut two 1/2" wide strips of tape about 1/2" less than the height of your cell phone case. Apply them to both long sides of the case, folding the strips over to hold the two sides together. To finish the bottom corners, cut six 1/2" by 1/2" squares and tape three around each corner.

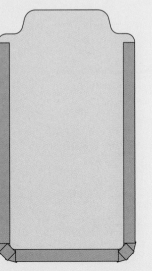

4 Unleash your inner designer and decorate!

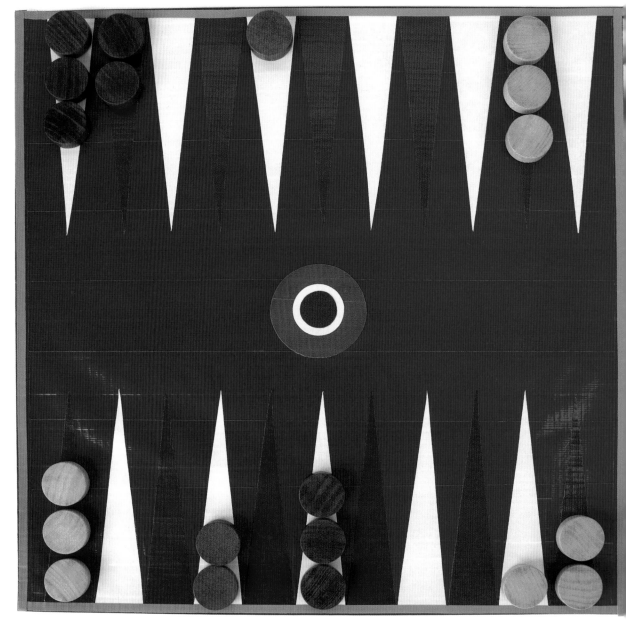

games on board

designed in ancient times to combat the boredom of, well, ancient times, board games haven't really changed much over the years. We still play 'em like the pharaohs did: a roll of the dice, two opposing sides, get to the other end of the board, conquer the castle. Equal parts strategy and luck, checkers and backgammon are examples of boredom-busting board games whose rules, look and appeal have stood the test of time. This fun twist on these classics replaces the typical board with lightweight duct tape playing surfaces that can be rolled up for easy toting. Use stones, buttons or coins for the playing pieces (avoid pieces of candy, unless you like fast games). Acey-deucy, king me, game on!

What You'll Need

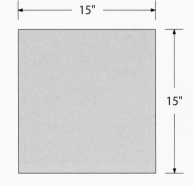

15"

15"

Sheet (Game Board)
×1

Make a 15" x 15" sheet for the board (see "How to Make Duct Tape Sheets" on page 8). Choose a color that will contrast with the points (for backgammon) and squares (for checkers).

1 Depending on how many unsealed edges you have after cutting and making your sheet, cut two or four 15" x ½" strips of tape and fold equally over each unsealed side.

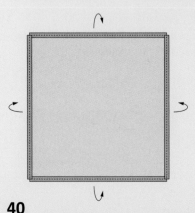

2 For the backgammon board, choose two colors of tape for the points. Cut eleven 1 ¼" x 5 ½" pieces of tape in both colors. To make the points, mark the middle of each piece along the width at the bottom and cut from this point to either corner at the top to make a triangle.

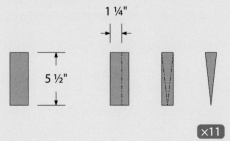

1 ¼"

5 ½"

×11

40

3 Tape the first point on the board, ⅝" in from the left side and flush with the bottom. Then tape a different colored point to the right of the first, corners touching. Repeat, alternating colors, for the nine remaining points across the bottom of the board. Next complete the top of the board, beginning at the top left with the alternate color of the bottom left point.

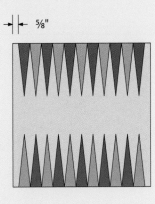

⅝"

4 To decorate, create a design to put in the middle and add a 15" x ½" decorative border around all sides.

5 For the checkers board, cut 32 1 ¾" x 1 ¾" squares of different colored tape than that of your board. (The color of the board will become the other colored square.)

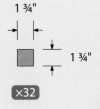

1 ¾"

1 ¾"

×32

6 Tape the first square ½" in from the left side and ½" up from the bottom of the sheet. Tape the next square 1 ¾" (or one square) to the right of the first. Complete the bottom row, then begin the next row one square in. The corners of the squares should touch, forming a grid.

½"

½"

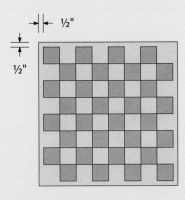

out
to lunch

i

In Japan you eat lunch out of a handsome, lacquered bento box. In India you bring your midday meal to work in a stacking set of interlocking, stainless steel tins called a tiffin. Here in the Western world? If you're a kid, you probably pack your PB&Js in the latest aluminum tie-in special (Canadian factoid: the aluminum lunch box was invented in 1954 by Sudbury, Ontario miner Leo May, after he accidentally sat on and crushed his tin one), but if you're an adult you probably brown bag it. Recapture your lost youth and become the envy of your lunch mates with this vibrant, lightweight, spill-proof lunch tote. If you're the imaginative type, you'll want to try making the handle and strap from different colors or patterns.

What You'll Need

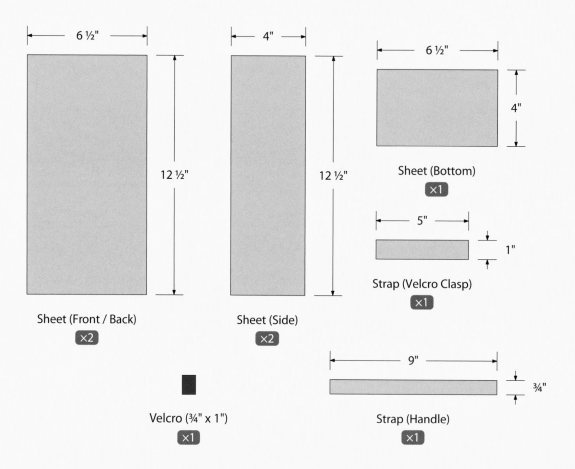

6 ½"

4"

6 ½"

4"

12 ½"

12 ½"

Sheet (Bottom)
×1

5"

1"

Strap (Velcro Clasp)
×1

Sheet (Front / Back)
×2

Sheet (Side)
×2

Velcro (¾" x 1")
×1

9"

¾"

Strap (Handle)
×1

Make the sheets for the front, back, sides, and bottom of the lunch bag (see "How to Make Duct Tape Sheets" on page 8). Also make the straps for the handle and clasp (see "How to Make Duct Tape Straps" on page 10).

1 Measuring 4" down from the top on either side, cut the back sheet in two along its width, creating two pieces measuring 6 ½" x 4" and 6 ½" x 8 ½".

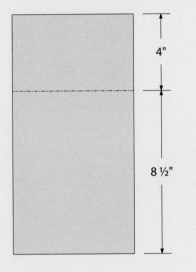

4"

8 ½"

2 Carefully fold the handle into a "U" shape and tape it to the larger back piece you cut in Step 1, so that the ends of the handle are 1 ½" in from either side and about 1" down from the top. This will be the inside of the bag. Then tape the strap for the clasp to the larger back piece, between the ends of the handle and 1" down from the top. Run a piece of tape across the handle and strap to secure them both in place.

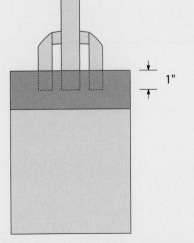

1"

3 Place the smaller, 6 ½" x 4" back piece you cut in Step 1 along the original cut line, atop the handle and strap. Run a piece of tape along the cut line to tape the two pieces back together. Flip the back over and run two pieces of tape above and below where the handle and strap come out to hide the cut line and strengthen the seam. You can overlap these pieces of tape slightly, but you will have to cut the pieces of tape down along the handle and strap so the tape can fold down.

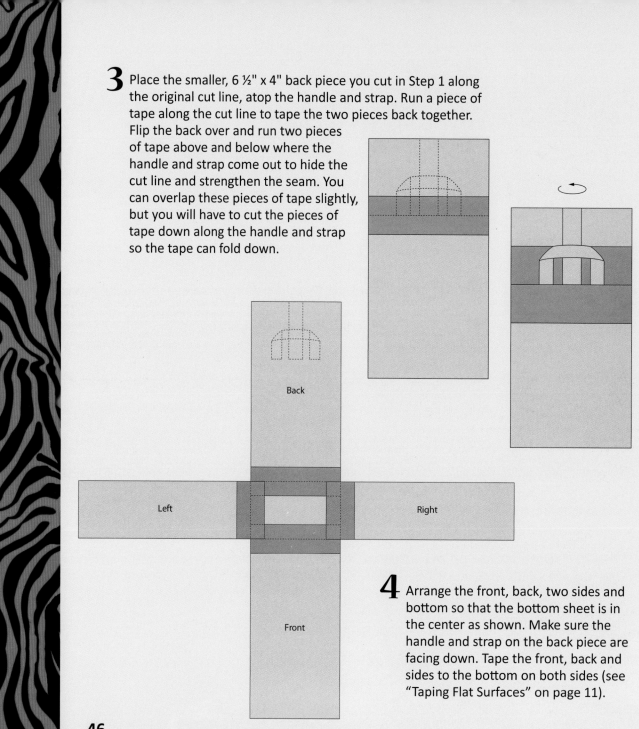

Back

Left

Right

Front

4 Arrange the front, back, two sides and bottom so that the bottom sheet is in the center as shown. Make sure the handle and strap on the back piece are facing down. Tape the front, back and sides to the bottom on both sides (see "Taping Flat Surfaces" on page 11).

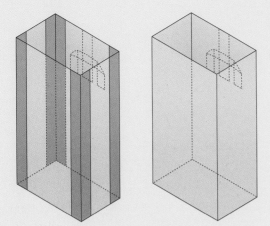

5 Carefully fold up the front, back and sides and tape the corners of the bag together, taping the seams inside and out (see "Taping Right-Angle Flat Surfaces" on page 11).

6 Stick a small piece of self-adhesive Velcro on the underside of the clasp. Roll the top of the bag down along its front until the end of the clasp is about halfway down the bag, and place the matching piece of Velcro on the bag underneath. Pack your lunch!

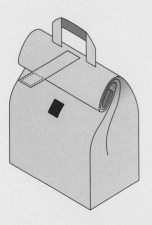
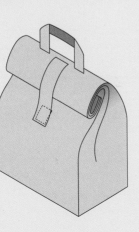

the spill master

Any parent or shellfish lover will instantly spot the utility in this project. Not only does it keep out the pureed carrots and lobster juices, it's waterproof, colorful and has a pocket to keep coveted food items, cutlery or toys. The roots of the word "bib" are actually a matter of some dispute: either it comes from the verb bibben ("to drink," natch), or it just sounded like Junior's babbling at feeding time. No matter, with this duct tape wonder you can get messy and tackle the dribbles with style and panache. Add a lead lining and you just might be able to wear it on your next visit to the dentist.

What You'll Need

11"

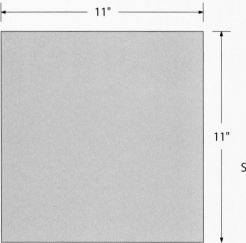

11"

11"

3 ½"

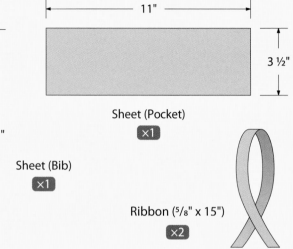

Sheet (Pocket)

×1

Sheet (Bib)

×1

Ribbon (⁵/₈" x 15")

×2

Make an 11" x 11" sheet for the bib and an 11" x 3 ½" sheet for the pocket (see "How to Make Duct Tape Sheets" on page 8).

1 Carefully draw the outline of the bib onto the square sheet using the dimensions provided and cut out.

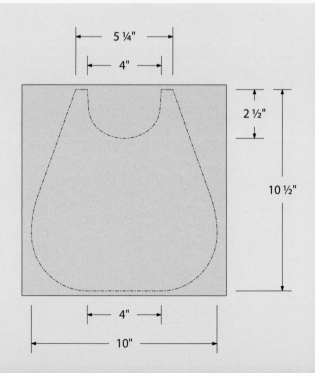

5 ¼"

4"

2 ½"

10 ½"

4"

10"

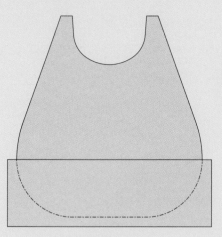

2 Using the bib as a guide, trace the outline of the bib's bottom curve onto the pocket sheet, then cut the pocket to shape.

3 To secure the pocket to the bib, cut 1" x ⅜" rectangles and fold them over the edges along the bottom and top of the pocket, overlapping the rectangles slightly. You can use a different color tape to liven things up if you like.

4 Flip the bib over and tape on two pieces of ⅝" ribbon to the top corners. The length of the ribbon is up to you; start with 15" and shorten as needed. Last, if cutting all those little squares doesn't drive you crazy, you can finish edging the bib as in Step 3. Decorate!

'And what enormous flowers they must be!' was
her next idea. 'Something like cottages with the
roofs taken off, and stalks put to them – and what
185

kleenex crib

Kimberley-Clark originally introduced the Kleenex facial tissue in the 1920s as a way to remove cold cream. Many customers, however, took their cue from the Japanese (who had been hip to blowing their noses in soft, silky paper as early as the 17th century), finding these new tissues equally useful for dealing with nosebleeds, the sniffles, or major weepy spells. It wasn't long before people wanted to show off this modern, practical household item and found new "homes" for it. Indeed, why settle for the uninspired designs of generic tissue boxes you see at the supermarket when you can make your own duct tape crib for your Kleenex? The project below is sized for a powder-room-sized box of tissues, but can easily be adapted to larger, the-whole-family-has-the-flu boxes.

What You'll Need

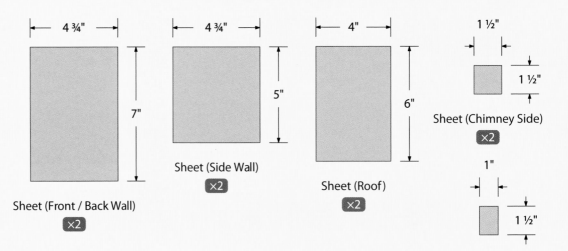

4 ¾"

7"

Sheet (Front / Back Wall)

×2

4 ¾"

5"

Sheet (Side Wall)

×2

4"

6"

Sheet (Roof)

×2

1 ½"

1 ½"

Sheet (Chimney Side)

×2

1"

1 ½"

Sheet (Chimney Front / Back)

×2

Make two sheets for the front and back walls of the house, two sheets for the side walls, and two sheets for the roof (see "How to Make Duct Tape Sheets" on page 8). Also cut two sheets for the front and back of the chimney and two sheets for the chimney sides.

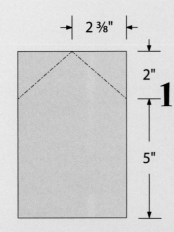

2 ⅜"

2"

5"

1 Mark the middle point on the top edge of the front wall sheet, 2 ⅜" in from either side. Next, measure and mark 2" down from the top on either side. Draw and cut diagonal lines from the middle point to these points. Repeat for the back wall sheet.

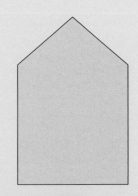

×2

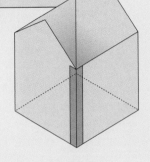

2 Line up the wall sheets, alternating front and back walls with side walls as shown. Tape the seams on one side, then flip and tape the seams on the other side (see "Taping Flat Surfaces" on page 11). Fold each taped join around to form a box, then tape the last seam together (see "Taping Right-Angle Flat Surfaces" on page 11).

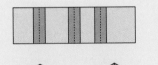

3 For the chimney, line up the sheets, alternating front and back walls with side walls, tape the seams together and form a small box as you did in Step 2. Finish the chimney by folding small, ½" wide strips of tape over the top edges.

4 Tape the two roof sheets together along their longest sides, then lay the roof flat with the taped seam running vertically. In the middle of the taped roof sheets, carefully cut out a hole for the chimney measuring 1 ⅜" x 1 ½", centered on the seam and with the longer side of the hole parallel with the longest side of the roof.

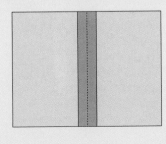

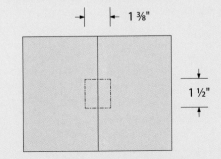

1 ⅜"

1 ½"

5 Fold the roof along the taped seam and place atop the box built in Steps 1 to 2. Secure the roof to the walls by taping it to the top edge of the box on the inside. Insert the chimney in the hole in the roof about ¼" down. To secure the chimney, flip the project upside-down and tape the chimney to the underside of the roof.

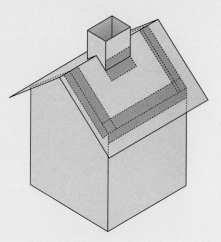

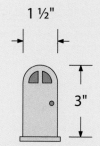

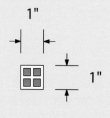

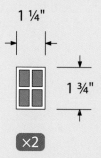

×2

6 Decorate your house with windows and doors cut out of different-colored duct tape. The windows measure 1" x 1" for the front and 1 ¼" x 1 ¾" for the side; the door is 1 ½" x 3". Add as much architectural detail as you like. To get that real glass look, use clear duct tape! Place the house over a box of tissues, pull one out through the roof, then wait for the next sneeze.

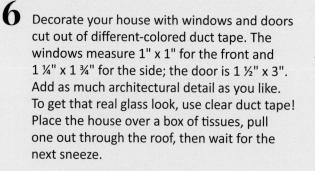

NAME:

ADDRESS:

PHONE #:

Bag Tag

As any seasoned traveler can tell you, most traveling bags look alike (yes, business class, that means you too). Yet, to identify them and tell 'em apart, people use little square luggage tags — that all look the same. No wonder airport baggage carousels are little merry-go-rounds of controlled chaos! Luckily, with a bit of the tape you can craft unique tags that can be easily spotted wherever your luggage happens to roll. A couple of tips: use strong ribbon or a chain to prevent the plane, train or bus gremlins from pinching your tag and adding it to their collection; and choose a design unique to you — we chose a penguin because they have a pretty unerring sense of direction, don't get lost and, well, look like little butlers. Who better to handle our luggage?

What You'll Need

5 ½"

6"

Make the two sheets (front/back) about ½" larger than your final tag design.

3 ½"

4"

Sheet (Front / Back)
×2

Clear Plastic Sheet
×1

1 Draw a penguin shape on one of the sheets. Stack the two sheets and, holding them together with fold-back clips or tape, cut out two identical shapes.

×2

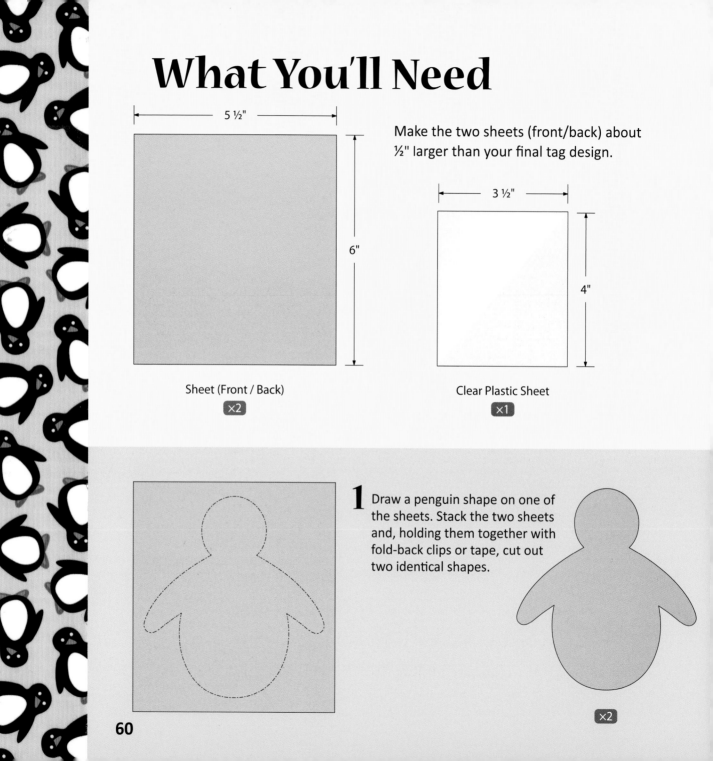

2 Cut an oval out of one of the shapes, leaving ½" around the penguin's body for the border.

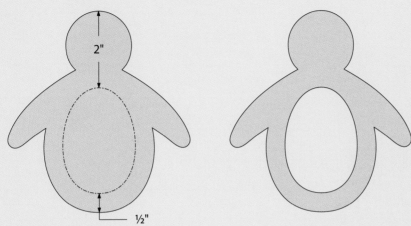

3 Cut a piece of rigid clear plastic slightly larger then the oval you cut in Step 2. Flip the shape over and secure the plastic to the shape using small overlapping pieces of tape.

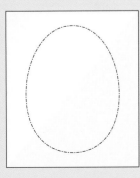

4 For the penguin's feet, cut out 1" x 1" triangles with rounded corners from small pieces of double-sided tape. Tape the feet to the bottom edge of the shape you cut in Step 2, on the same side as the plastic, about 1" apart.

5 Place the two penguin shapes back together, making sure they are aligned. Using small pieces of overlapping tape, seal all the edges (see "Taping Curved Edges" on page 12). Stop taping at the outer edge of either foot to leave the opening for an ID tag. To get a smooth surface for the face and arms, use single pieces of duct tape to hide the over-lapping tape and cut off the excess around the shape. Add eyes and a beak.

6 Punch a hole through both sheets of the tag at the bottom, between the feet. Insert your ID card between the sheets and attach a ribbon or chain so you can secure it to your luggage.

FULL-SIZE TEMPLATE

wild wild vest

The Brits call it a waistcoat, while we know it as one-third of a three-piece suit. The vest has been around since the 1600s, when King Charles II of England decided to make a fashion statement by wearing one under his coat. The fringed leather vest has become synonymous with cowboys and rodeos; our rough-hewn, handsome duct tape design would be right home at a hootenanny or out on the frontier. There's lots of measuring in this project, but the results are worth it!

What You'll Need

To make the front and back sheets, measure around your chest, add 1" to 2" for room and divide by two. This will be the width of each sheet (A). Measure from the top middle of your shoulder to the top of your hips; this will be the length of the back sheet (B). Add 2" to this measurement to get the length of the front sheet (C).

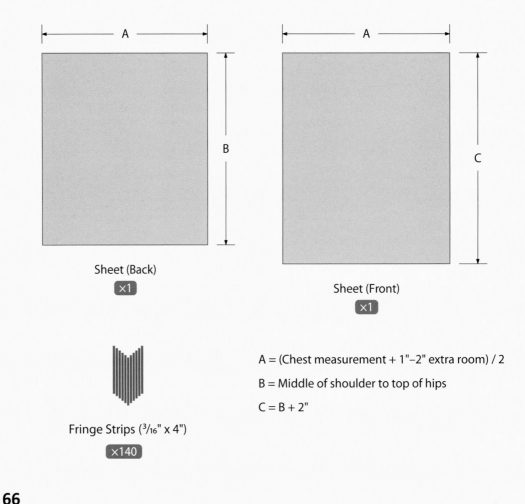

Sheet (Back)
×1

Sheet (Front)
×1

Fringe Strips (³/₁₆" x 4")
×140

A = (Chest measurement + 1"–2" extra room) / 2

B = Middle of shoulder to top of hips

C = B + 2"

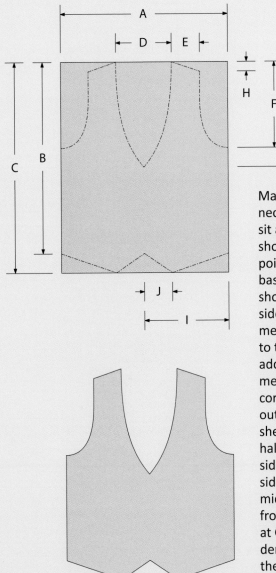

1

Mark out the cuts on the front sheet first. For the neck opening, each side of the opening should sit at the base of your neck where it meets your shoulder (D). Measure equally from the center point out. For the shoulders, measure from the base of your neck to about halfway across your shoulder. Add this measurement (E) on either side of your neck opening (D). For the arm holes, measure from the top middle of your shoulder to the middle of the underside of your armpit; adding 1" to 2" for extra room. Mark this measurement (F) on either side of the sheet, from the top corners down. Next, cut straight down from the outer E mark curving towards F on the edge of the sheet. Once the cut is complete, fold the sheet in half lengthwise and trace this curve onto the other side of the vest. Make a matching cut on the other side. To cut out the neck opening, mark G at the midpoint of the sheet and cut a V shape starting from either side of D, curving slightly and ending at G in the middle of the vest. To angle the shoulders, from the outer E marks mark down 1" from the top edge of the sheet (H), draw a line back to the inner E marks and cut. Mark 2" up from the bottom on each side and 2" up in the center across the width of the sheet. On each half of the sheet (I), mark ⅓ of I from the center out (J). Cut from mark J on an angle up to the 2" mark in the center and up to the 2" mark on the side. Repeat for the other bottom side of the vest.

2 For the back of the vest, place the front sheet on top of it and align at the top edge. Trace and mark out measurements D, E, F and H. Remove the front sheet. Measure down 1 ½" from the midpoint of the top edge of the sheet (K). Draw a curve the width of D with the center height of K. Mark ¾" on either side of the bottom midpoint of the sheet (L) and mark 2" up from the bottom midpoint. Cut out a triangle from these points. Cut out a vest shape for the back of the vest.

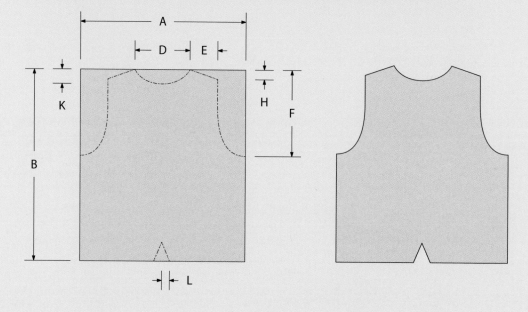

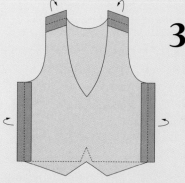

3 Place the front sheet on top of the back. Align and tape the top shoulders and sides inside and out. Make a cut up the center of the front sheet of the vest for the opening.

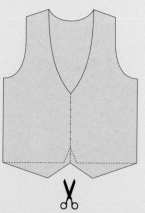

68

4 Tape around all the cut edges of the vest (see "Taping Curved Edges" on page 12).

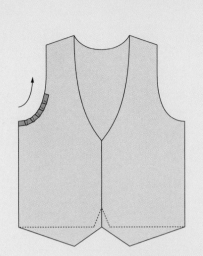

5 Make the fringe by cutting strips of $3/16$" wide double-sided tape approximately 4" in length (this will vary depending on the size of the vest). Lay out the fringe on an angle — with each piece of fringe slightly lower — in a V shape on the front. Tape the fringe in sections, then cover all tape pieces with one long length of tape to hide. Repeat on the back of the vest.

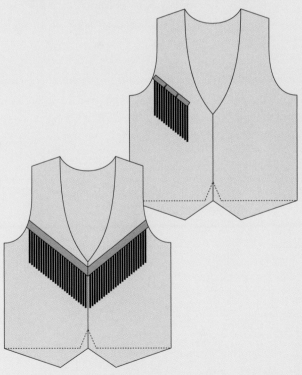

cheeky chaps

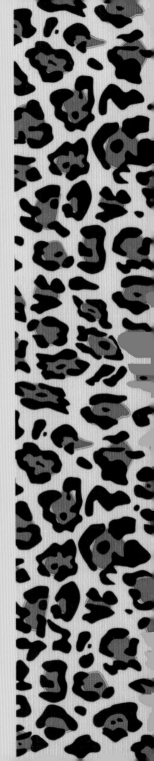

Standard issue for cattle drivers, rodeo riders, bikers and the leather crowd, chaps were originally designed to protect the legs from stampeding cattle and livestock, thorny vegetation like cacti and sagebrush and the harsh elements out on the range. Named after Mexican chaparejos, they were almost always made out of leather or animal hide. We're pleased to say that no animals were harmed in the making of the chaps in this project, for they rely on the tougher-than-leather resiliency of duct tape. The straight-and-narrow variety, called shotgun or stovepipe chaps, is commonly seen on Canadian ranches and at rodeos, and they're pretty darned easy to make, so saddle up!

What You'll Need

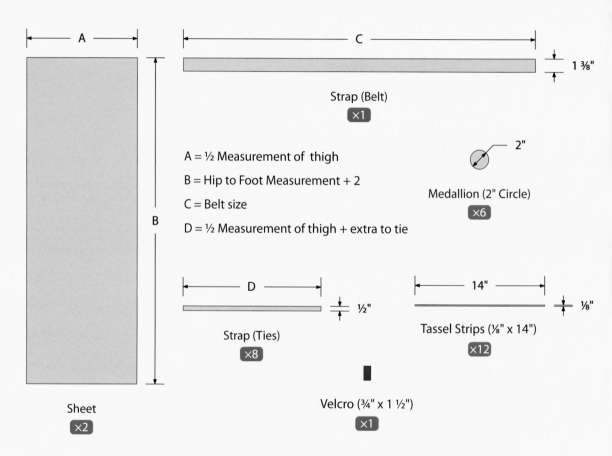

A ————

B

Sheet
×2

C ————————————

1 ⅜"

Strap (Belt)
×1

A = ½ Measurement of thigh
B = Hip to Foot Measurement + 2
C = Belt size
D = ½ Measurement of thigh + extra to tie

2"

Medallion (2" Circle)
×6

D ————

½"

Strap (Ties)
×8

14" ————

⅛"

Tassel Strips (⅛" x 14")
×12

Velcro (¾" x 1 ½")
×1

To determine measurements for the sheets, first measure the circumference of your thigh and divide by two (A). Next measure from your hip to the top of your foot and add 2" for a belt loop (B). These measurements will be the width and length of your sheets; make two. If you find the length of the sheet too long to make easily, divide it in half and make two smaller sheets to tape together (see "Taping Flat Surfaces" on page 11).

1 To make the chap legs, first measure from your belly button to the outside of your leg (E). Then measure from your hip to halfway down your thigh and add 2" for the belt loop (F). Take the first sheet you prepared in What You'll Need and with the visible side face up, from the top left corner measure in and mark the first measurement (E). From the top right corner, measure down and mark the second measurement (F). Draw a smooth curve that connects the two marks as shown and cut out. Repeat for the second sheet by using the first sheet as a guide to trace on the curve. Make sure both curves are in the center when you place the two chap legs side by side.

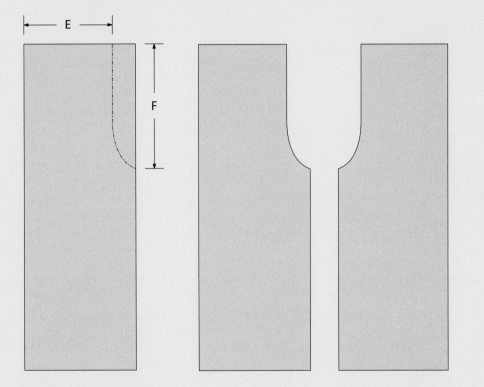

E = Navel to outer seam

F = Hip to halfway down thigh + 2"

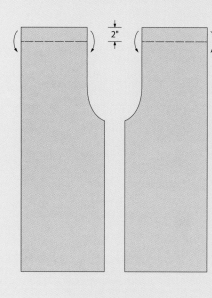

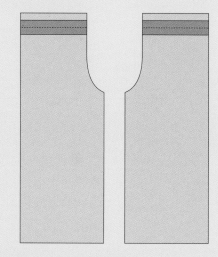

2 At the top of each chap leg, fold over the top 2" to form the belt loop that you accommodated for in What You'll Need and Step 1. Fold onto the back of the legs and tape across.

3 To make the ties, use cutoffs from other projects or the pieces you cut out from the chap legs in Step 1 if they are long enough. The ties need to be about ½" wide by half the circumference of your leg, plus a little extra to tie (D). Make eight ties and tape four to the back of each chap leg, two on either side, just below the curve, and two around the middle of your calves. Secure them with square pieces of tape. Also place a small piece of tape on the front of the chaps covering each tie and part of the chap leg. Cut the excess tape away from the tie. This will prevent the tie from pulling away from the leg.

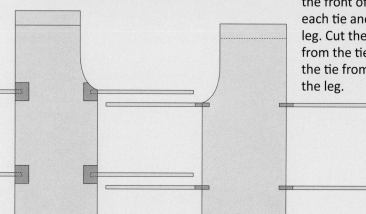

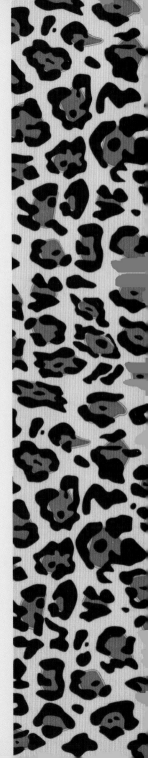

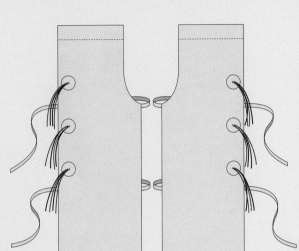

¼"

4 To make the medallions, cut six 2" diameter circles from small sheets of single-sided (sticky) duct tape. Place the medallions on the outside part of the leg within the top two thirds of the chaps. After you have stuck them down where you want, cut two slits ¼" apart (like an electrical outlet) in the middle of the medallions and through the chap legs. To make the tassels, cut 12 separate ⅛" x 14" strips from double-sided (non-sticky) pieces of tape. Make six of one color and six of another. Run two tassels for each medallion through the front of the medallion and chap leg, then loop around back through the second slit. Secure by wrapping a thin piece of tape around the tassels near the medallion on the outside of the chaps.

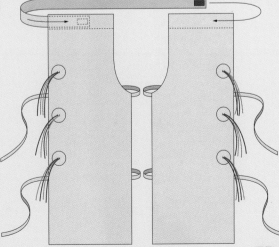

5 To make a belt, cut a 1" strap (see "Making Duct Tape Straps" on page 10) the size of your waist (C) and run it through the belt loop. Add Velcro or snaps to either end of the belt loop, following the instructions provided.

sassy skirt

a simple utilitarian garment dating back to at least 3,900 BC, the skirt has long been a trusty bellwether for fashion and culture, its length rising and falling with the times: from long (Dior's "New Look" in the late 1940s) to short (the miniskirt in the 1960s). A myriad of skirt trends — ballerinas, pencils, poodles, dirndls, sarongs, scooters — have come and gone (and come back again), but the skirt remains a staple wardrobe item in the Western world. Unleash your inner clothier with this simple A-line with ruffle pattern made from this season's hottest fabric: duct tape. Jean Paul Gaultier would be proud.

What You'll Need

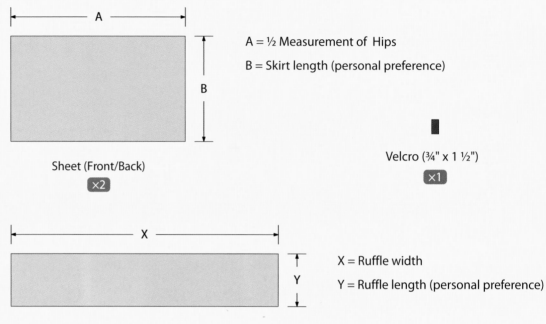

A = ½ Measurement of Hips

B = Skirt length (personal preference)

Sheet (Front/Back)
×2

Velcro (¾" x 1 ½")
×1

X = Ruffle width

Y = Ruffle length (personal preference)

Sheet (Ruffles)

To determine the dimensions of the sheets for your skirt, first measure around your hips and divide in half. This will be the width of your skirt (A). Also decide on the length of your skirt (B) (usually about halfway down your thigh). Keep in mind that you will be adding a ruffle to the skirt and this will increase the length (about ⅓ of the skirt's length). Make two sheets to these specifications for the front and the back. For the ruffles sheet, see Step 5.

1 Measure your waist and divide by two (C). Subtract this measurement from the width of your sheets. Divide the result by two. Mark this measurement in from both top corners of your front sheet. Stack the front and back sheets and, holding them together with fold-back clips or tape, cut from the top marks to the bottom corners of the sheets.

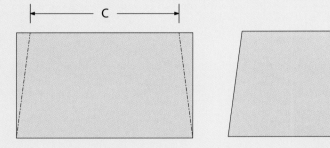

C = ½ Measurement of Waist

2 Tape each side of the skirt inside and out (see "Taping Flat Surfaces" on page 11).

3 At the back of your skirt in the middle, use scissors to make a vertical cut down from the top, a little less then half the length of your skirt. Sandwich one edge of your cut between two pieces of tape, creating a tab the length of your cut with an overhang of about 1". (You may want to double this up with tape for strength.) Following the instructions included, add self-adhesive Velcro to the top of this tab and to the other side of the cut on the inside, and align.

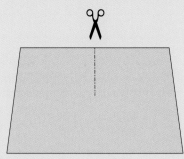

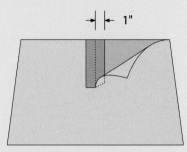

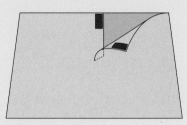

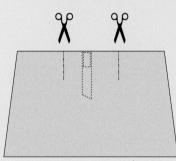

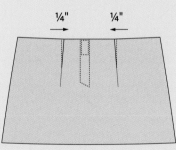

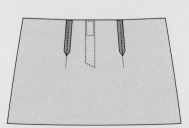

4 You may need to pull in the waist of your skirt if it does not fit as tightly as you like. To do this, cut an even number of small slits down the front and back. Measure out evenly from the center outwards. The number of slits will depend on how much tighter you want your skirt to be. Bring the slits ¼" on top of one another and tape down the length, inside and out.

5 The dimensions of the sheet for the ruffle will depend on your skirt size, but its height (Y) should be around ⅓ of the skirt's length. To help figure out the length (X) of the sheet, account for 1" to 2" for each ruffle fold times the number of folds you want to make. You can make the ruffle in separate sheets and tape them together as you go. (This way you don't have to worry about making it too short.) Tape the ruffle to the inside of the skirt first, making 1" folds all going in the same direction. Tape each fold of your sheet separately. Run a larger piece of tape over all the smaller ones to secure them in place.

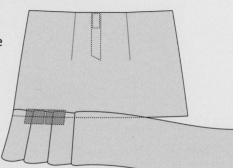

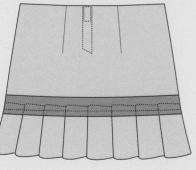

6 On the outside, run long pieces of tape around the seam between the ruffle and top portion of the skirt.

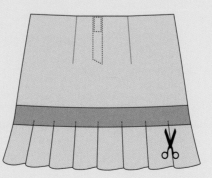

7 Cut the tape along the pleats to allow the tape to lay flat. Decorate!

backpack

the original hands-free organizer, backpacks have been a mainstay of mountaineers, soldiers, campers and cyclists around the world, but are most commonly identified with school and students. Indeed, a sturdy backpack is a schoolkid's best friend, home to their textbooks, mobile devices, teacher's apples, homework, geometry sets and pencil cases. This simple, curved backpack project with two zippered compartments can be customized for any number of different grade levels — you can go basic black and industrial or decorate it with a fun animal face for younger schoolkids.

What You'll Need

Make sheets for the front, back, bottom and sides of the backpack.

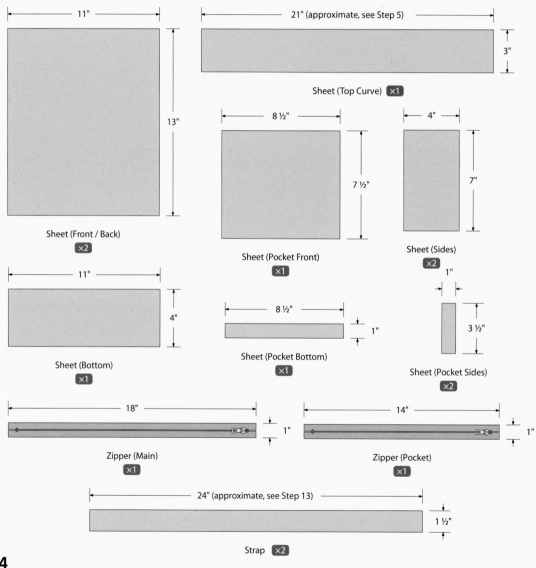

11"

13"

Sheet (Front / Back)
×2

21" (approximate, see Step 5)

3"

Sheet (Top Curve) ×1

8 ½"

7 ½"

Sheet (Pocket Front)
×1

4"

7"

Sheet (Sides)
×2

11"

4"

Sheet (Bottom)
×1

8 ½"

1"

Sheet (Pocket Bottom)
×1

1"

3 ½"

Sheet (Pocket Sides)
×2

18"

1"

Zipper (Main)
×1

14"

1"

Zipper (Pocket)
×1

24" (approximate, see Step 13)

1 ½"

Strap ×2

1 Take the back sheet and make marks halfway across the top width and 5" down the sides from the top corners. Connect the marks with a half circle as evenly as possible. Cut the curved top. Aligning the back and front sheets at the bottom, trace and cut out the curve on the front sheet.

5 ½"   5 ½"

5"

×2

2 Cut four 1 ½" horizontal slits on the back sheet for the straps, 2" in from either side of the sheet. Measure 2" up from the bottom of the sheet for the lower slits and 9 ½" from the bottom for the upper slits.

9 ½"

2"

1 ½"   2"

3 Tape the front, back and side sheets to the bottom sheet as shown. Tape on both sides.

4 Fold up the front, back and side sheets and tape the corners inside and out (see "Taping Right-Angle Flat Surfaces" on page 11).

1 ½"

1 ½"

4"

5 Make a sheet for the top: measure the curve you cut in Step 1 with a sewing tape measure, and make the sheet a few inches longer than this measurement. To attach the zipper, cut the top sheet in half lengthwise. Center an 18" long zipper between the two halves of the sheet and parallel to them, and tape over the cloth part of the zipper and the two halves of the top sheet so that the resulting assembly is 4" wide. Flip over and repeat for the reverse side. Tape the ends of the zipper and sheets on both sides as well. You should now have a 21" (approximate) x 4" rectangular sheet for the top of the backpack. (If the zipper is too loose, you can sew it in place after this step and cover again with more duct tape.)

6 Center the top sheet with the zipper on top of the curve of the backpack. Pull down each side of the top sheet to the sides of the backpack to make sure the lengths are accurate, and tack down with a couple pieces of tape. Trim if necessary.

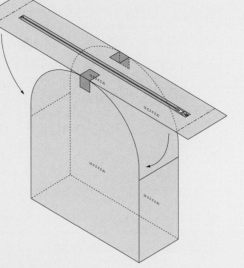

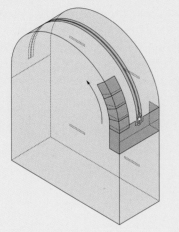

7 Tape each end of the top sheet to the sides of the backpack inside and out. Tape all around the curve of the backpack on the front and back sides with small overlapping pieces of tape, taping inside and out (see "Taping Curved Edges" on page 13).

8 Make the sheets for the front pocket front, bottom and sides. Measure halfway across the top width of the front sheet and 4"down each side. Draw and cut a curve in the pocket front as you did in Step 1.

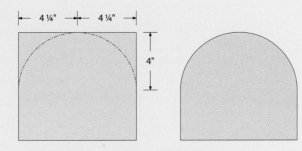

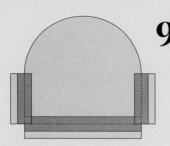 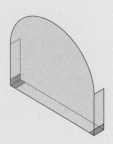

9 Take the side and bottom sheets for the front pocket and tape them to the front pocket sheet as shown (see "Taping Flat Surfaces" on page 11). Fold the sides and bottom and tape inside and out where the corners meet (see "Taping Right-Angle Flat Surfaces" on page 11).

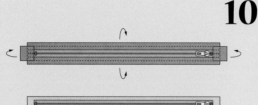

10 Cover the fabric of a 14" zipper on both sides with duct tape. Trim off the excess so that the zipper remains the same width as before you put the duct tape on. Leave excess tape on both ends of the zipper and trim after. Tape the ends of the zipper as you did in Step 5.

11 Attach the zipper to the front pocket as you did in Step 6, taping around one curved edge only.

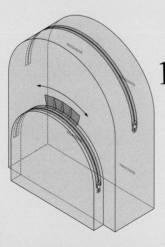

12 Tape the front pocket to the front of the backpack, flush with the bottom, using small overlapping pieces of tape (see "Taping Curved Edges" on page 12). (If you are using different colors of tape for the backpack and the pocket, tape the pocket on using the same color tape as the backpack, then cover the pieces of tape on the pocket with a thin strip the same color as the pocket.)

13 Make the straps (see "How to Make Duct Tape Straps" on page 10) to fit the size of the backpack owner, using a sewing tape measure to gauge how much strap you will need. Run the straps through the slits in the back of the backpack and tape the ends together. You may also want to tape the straps to the back sheet on the inside of the backpack so that they don't slide around.

14 To make animal ears, cut out the ear shape you want, with a flat edge at the bottom. Fold one bottom edge on top of the other in a triangular shape (this will form a mini cone shape at the bottom and allow the ear to stand upright). Tape together and then secure to the top of the backpack. If you like, decorate the front of the backpack with a fun animal face!

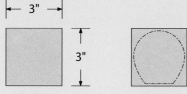

small-scale monster

He hails from the briny deep and is known by many names: Jörmungandr, the Norse Serpent; Leviathan, the sea monster from Biblical times; the famous Loch Ness Monster; Yacumama from the Amazon; and Ogopogo from Canada's Okanagan Lake. Green, fearsome and fun, this sea monster puppet is just the thing for kids' parties, impromptu puppet shows, long car trips or for getting you a seat on the subway. You can create intricate designs with the scales, and the basic shape can be adapted to create other serpentine puppet designs — shed the fins and keep the forked tongue and you have a snake!

What You'll Need

Make sheets for the puppet's top, bottom, mouth and fins (see "How To Make Duct Tape Sheets" on page 8).

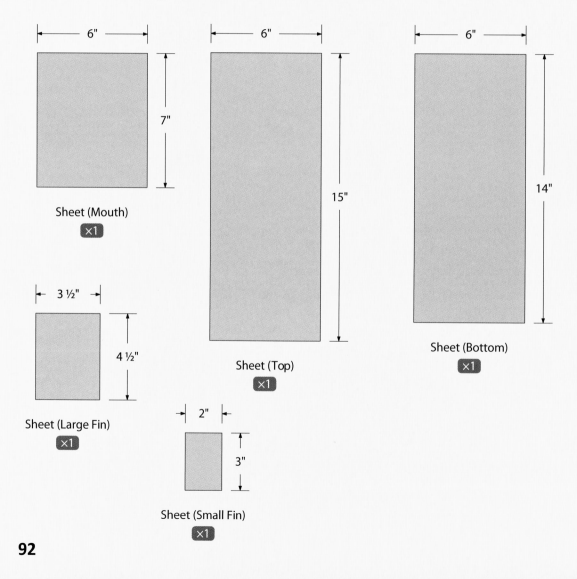

6"

7"

Sheet (Mouth)
×1

6"

15"

Sheet (Top)
×1

6"

14"

Sheet (Bottom)
×1

3 ½"

4 ½"

Sheet (Large Fin)
×1

2"

3"

Sheet (Small Fin)
×1

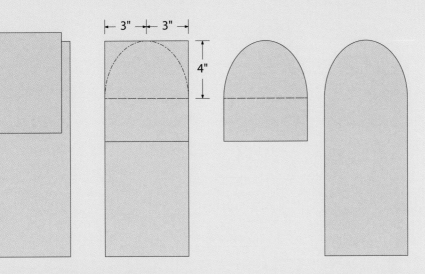

1 Stack and align the ends of top sheet and mouth sheet. Measure and mark 4" down on either side of the mouth sheet from the top corners and fold. Also mark the top center across the width. Holding the sheets together with fold-back clips or tape, draw and cut an even curve out of both sheets ending at the 4" marks on either side.

2 Flip the mouth sheet around and stack it atop the bottom sheet so its straight end is aligned with the top edge of the bottom sheet. Draw and cut an even curve ending at the fold mark made in Step 1. The mouth sheet should now be somewhat oval shaped.

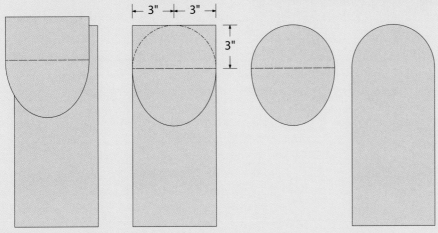

3 Take the bottom sheet and mouth sheet from Step 2 and tape them together along the curved edges at the top with a series of overlapping pieces of duct tape (see "Taping Curved Edges" on page 12). Stop at the folds in the mouth sheet. Flip around and repeat with the top sheet and the other curved end of the mouth sheet. Again, tape until the fold in the mouth sheet. You should now have the top and bottom sheets attached to the oval mouth sheet.

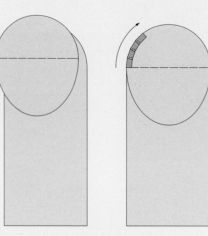

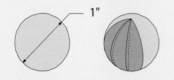

1"

4 Tape up each side of the puppet up to the points where you taped on the mouth sheet.

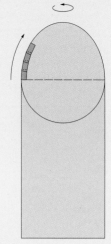

5 To make the eyeballs, crumple aluminum foil into two 1" diameter balls, rolling them around until they are really smooth. Cover with duct tape (see "Taping Curved Surfaces" on page 13). To tape the eyeballs onto the top of the puppet's head, cut a few small strips of tape for each eyeball. Tape half the length of the strip to the back of the eyeball at the base and the other half of the strip to the top of the head. Repeat until each eyeball is secure.

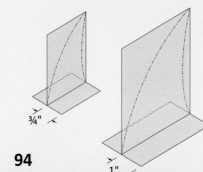

¾"

1"

6 To make the small and large fins, cover both sides of each fin sheet with another layer of duct tape that is 1" longer at the bottom. Do not let the extra lengths stick together — hold them apart by sticking each side onto your cutting surface as shown. (These will be used to attach the fins to the back of your puppet.) Use scissors to cut out a fin shape in each sheet. Tape the smaller fin on the back of the puppet just below the head and the larger fin below it.

7 Make the teeth from ½" x ½" double-sided squares of white tape, adding another, longer layer of tape to both sides as you did with the fins, to adhere the teeth to the inside of the mouth. Cut triangles for the teeth. After attaching the teeth to the inside of the mouth, cover the ends with tape the same color as the mouth.

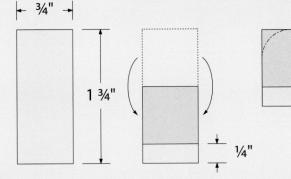

8 To make the scales, take a ¾" wide by 1 ¾" long piece of tape and fold it over onto itself lengthwise, leaving ¼" of sticky surface exposed at the bottom. Cut out a curve at the top of the scale. Start taping the scales at the bottom of the puppet, offsetting each new row to create a scale pattern. You can use different shades of the same color or go multicolored. Finish by decorating the fins, adding a tongue or whatever else you want!

this little piggy

though debit and credit are now the preferred methods of payment in North America, many of us still have the odd pile of change lying around. And so many of us will entrust this loose coinage to socks, mattresses, banks and piggy banks. "Why a pig?" you might reasonably ask. Is the pig a particularly parsimonious or spendthrift creature? Actually, once upon a time in the 17th century, these penny-saving banks didn't look like pigs at all — they were simply kitchen jars made from a clay called "pygg" in Middle English. Our little piggy is made from polka-dot patterned duct tape and a can with a removable lid (he's too cute to break to count your fortune).

What You'll Need

For the body, find a cardboard or plastic can with a lid about 5" in diameter. Try to find one that doesn't taper.

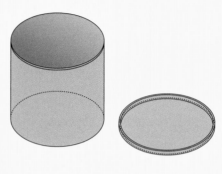

Cardboard Tube
×2

Can & Lid (~ 5" Diameter)
×1

1 With the exception of the bottom, cover the entire can — including the lid — with duct tape. Cut a $^3/_{16}$" x 1 ¼" coin slot in the middle of the side of the can.

2 To determine the size for the piggy's snout, measure the diameter of the can and set your compass to this measurement. This will create a circle double the diameter of your can (in our example, 10" in diameter). Make a duct tape sheet (see "Making Duct Tape Sheets" on page 8) at least 1" larger than this circle, then use the compass to draw the circle onto your sheet. Measure and draw a smaller circle (slightly less then half the diameter of the larger circle) in the center of the larger one, using the same center point. The smaller the inside circle, the pointier the snout will be. Mark out ¼ of the large circle by measuring from the midpoints of the bottom and side of the sheet. Cut out both circles and ¼ of the larger one. Save the inner circle.

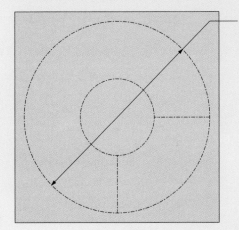

2 x Can Diameter

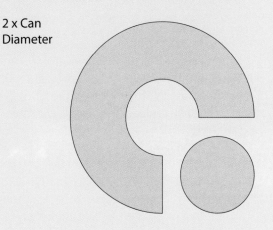

3 To make the snout, fold the large C-shaped circle into a cone, making sure it matches the diameter of your can. Tape the seam together inside and out.

4 For the nose, first measure the diameter of the smaller opening on the snout. Draw a circle with this diameter (A) with the compass on the inner circle you cut out in Step 2 (C), using the same center point. Then draw a second circle (B) 1" bigger in diameter than the first, again using the same center point. Cut out this last circle (B).

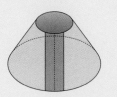

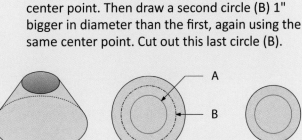

A

B

C

5 Cut an even number of small slits around the circle from the outside edge to the inner circle. You now have a series of tabs.

6 Place this tabbed circle on top of the snout. Folding down every other tab, insert them into the hole in the cone. Fold down the remaining tabs onto the surface of the snout and tape all around the nose to hold it securely in place (see "Taping Curved Surfaces" on page 13). Secure the inside tabs with tape as well. Cut a circle of sticky-sided duct tape to affix to the end of the snout and clean up all tape ends.

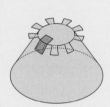

7 Tape the snout to the bottom of the can opposite the lid end (see "Taping Curved Edges" on page 12).

8 To make the legs, take two empty toilet paper rolls and cut each one in half. Cut down the length of the roll and tightly roll each piece so that it is 1" in diameter. Tape to secure. Cut the tops of all four rolls at a 45° angle, then cover each leg in duct tape. You can adjust the angle depending on how close or far apart you want the legs to be.

×4

9 Turn the piggy bank over so the coin slot is underneath. Tape each leg with the angled side to the body. When positioning the legs, space them evenly and remember the bank will be front-heavy because of the snout, so make sure the front is well supported. Use small strips of tape to tape around the top of the leg and the can (see "Taping Curved Edges" on page 12).

10 To add the finishing touches, cut out pointy ears from small sheets of duct tape. Fold the ears in half to create a pleat and tape them to the body near the snout. For the tail, wrap tape around a twist tie, curl it around and tape it to the lid of the can. Add eyes and nostrils, and start saving for retirement!

i ♥ u box

for over 2,000 years, since its discovery by the Mayans and Aztecs, chocolate has been a delectable delight for our tastebuds. Kurt Cobain of Nirvana even immortalized the traditional Valentine's Day gift in a song (although, incorrigible romantic that he was, he originally called the song "Heart-Shaped Coffin"). If you want to truly impress your sweetheart, mention that the latest research shows chocolate to be a powerful superfood in the fight against heart disease, and give him or her an assortment of caramel, nougat and coconut crèmes in this handsome heart-shaped box, for nothing says "Be my Valentine" like chocolates wrapped in duct tape.

What You'll Need

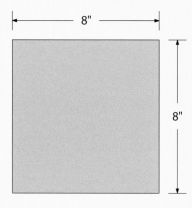

8"

8"

Sheet (Top / Bottom) ×2

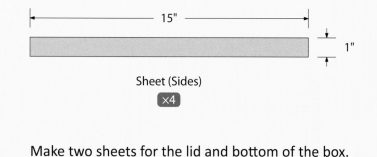

15"

1"

Sheet (Sides)
×4

Make two sheets for the lid and bottom of the box.

1 On the top sheet, draw a heart as symmetrically as possible. (Tip: Use a round object to trace the two curves at the top.) Stack the two sheets and, holding them together with fold-back clips or tape, cut out two identical heart shapes.

×2

2 To determine the length of the box sides, use a sewing tape measure to measure down either side of the heart, from the top dip to the bottom point. Make these measurements slightly longer, as you can always trim them afterwards. Cut four 1" wide sheets to this length, two for the top of the box, two for the bottom.

×4

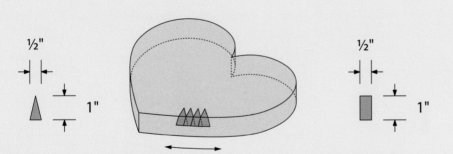

½"

1"

½"

1"

3 Secure the sides of the box to the lid using small triangles of contrasting-colored tape 1" tall and ½" wide at the base. You'll need to make a lot! Tape the tip of the triangle to the lid of the box and fold the base down onto the side. Overlap the triangles for strength and so that you can't see any holes (see "Taping Curved Edges" on page 12). Tape each side of the box onto the lid separately, starting at the top dip. Cut the excess length of the sides at the bottom, and secure them together at the dip and point of the heart with tape inside and out. To make the design even, cover the base of the triangles with a ½" wide piece of tape all around the outside of the box. For the bottom of the box, cut out ½" by 1" rectangles instead of triangles and repeat the process.

2"

4"

4 To make the roses, fold over a 4" piece of tape, leaving ¼" of the sticky surface exposed. Cut out a rounded shape as shown. Repeat this five to six times using white and red tape. Roll the first petal into a tight coil, using the sticky edge on the inside bottom to hold it together. Wrap another petal around the first, using the sticky edge to keep it in place. Keep adding petals, wrinkling them to keep them slightly uneven. (The outside petals don't have to be as tightly coiled as the first.) Bend back the top edge of the outermost petals after they are stuck on. After all the petals are attached, wrap a thin piece of tape around the bottom to secure them together. Secure the rose to the lid with loops of tape and small strips at the base.

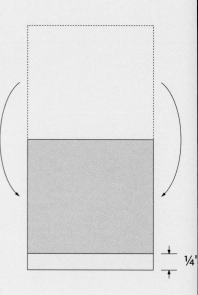

¼"

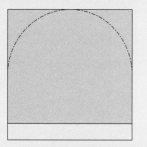

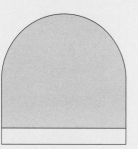

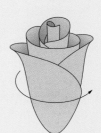

×6

5 For the leaves, cut out leaf shapes about 1" wide in the middle and 2" long. Pinch at one end, wrapping a thin piece of tape around the stem. Attach the leaves between the roses the same way you attached the roses to the lid. Fill with chocolates!

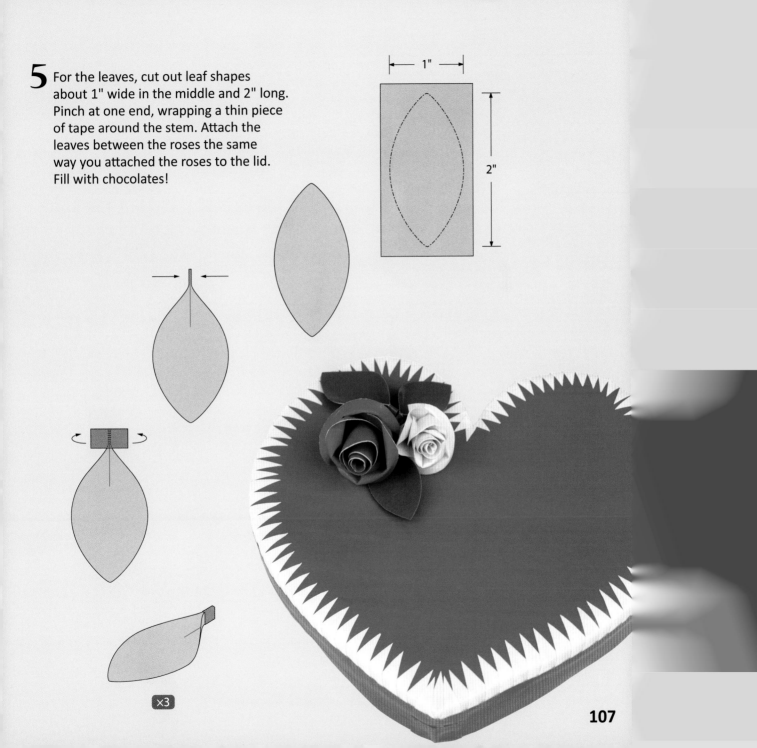

×3

yuletide tree topper

The Christmas tree originated in early modern Germany as a festive decoration and religious symbol. Today, holiday trees are topped with anything you like, from a family photo to an abstract design or even a company logo. Traditional tree toppers included the star, candles, Santa figures, and of course angels. To make things more fun for children, stories were told about angels decorating the trees and getting their hair caught in the branches, which accounted for draping of streamers, and later, tinsel. Here we've made a plain, white-and-gold style angel, but feel free to be creative with colors and patterns to fit your tree. You could even make it with clear duct tape if you want a Christmas light to shine out from underneath. Duct the halls with this lovely project, and have an angelic presence look over your family this yuletide season!

What You'll Need

Make two sheets for the tiered body, one for the bottom and another for the top.

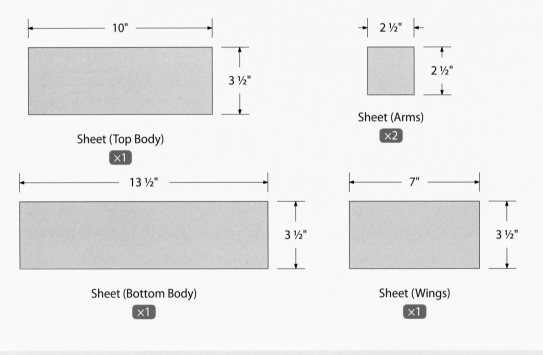

|← 10" →|

3 ½"

Sheet (Top Body)
×1

|← 2 ½" →|

2 ½"

Sheet (Arms)
×2

|← 13 ½" →|

3 ½"

Sheet (Bottom Body)
×1

|← 7" →|

3 ½"

Sheet (Wings)
×1

1 To make the body, add trim along the longest edge of the bottom sheet, folding it over the edge. Wrap the sheet lengthwise to form a circle, taping the two ends inside and out.

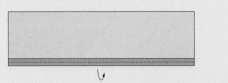

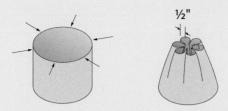

2 From the inside, pinch evenly around the top of the bottom circle six times, ½" in toward the center, and tape to hold. Repeat Steps 1 and 2 with the top part of the body.

3 Stack the top tier atop the bottom one and tape the two together from the inside.

4 For the head, roll a piece of aluminum foil into a ball around 1 ½" in diameter. Wrap the ball in one large piece of aluminum foil and twist the excess at the base of the ball to form a neck. Cover the head and neck with small pieces of tape (see "Taping Curved Surfaces" on page 13). Insert the neck through the top tier and secure it from the inside with tape. Wrap a thin piece of tape around the edge of the top tier to pull and tighten it around the neck.

1 ½"

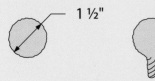

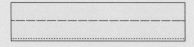

5 For the hair, cut a long piece of tape and fold it over along its length, leaving about ⅛" of sticky surface exposed. Cut between 50 and 75 ⅛" strips off the long folded piece of tape. Starting at the base and working up to the top, attach the strips around the back and sides of the head.

⅛"

⅛"

×75

6 To make the wings, fold the sheet in half along its width. Draw the wings with the fold in the center. Cut out the wings and tape onto the back top tier of the body.

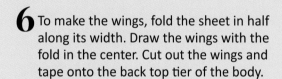

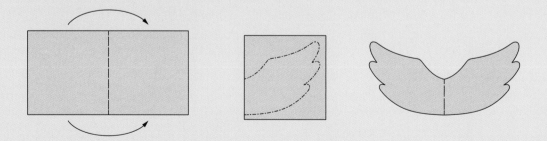

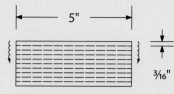

5"

³⁄₁₆"

7 For the halo, cut a 5" long piece of tape and fold over and over until it is ³⁄₁₆" wide. Fold into a ring and tape the ends together. Attach the ring to a toothpick wrapped in duct tape, then secure to the back of the head with tape.

8 For the arms, make two 2 ½" x 2 ½" square sheets. For each sheet, fold into a triangle and tape together to form a cone. Attach with tape to the top tier of the body between the pleats, then seat the angel atop your Christmas tree.

×2

bodacious bows

ah, the bow tie. The most inscrutable of fashion accessories. Is it a sign of suave, scholarly confidence or a nerd talisman? Favored by magicians, clowns, accountants and newspaper editors, it's also been rocked by some cool kids from Glee and well, "Black Tie" wouldn't be black tie without it. (And, just like neckties, there are no doubt skinny-versus-wide debates raging on somewhere.) In the end, a bow tie is really in how you wear it, so let's signal funky and fun with these one-of-a-kind duct tape styles. Don't worry about all that complicated tying of bat wings and butterflies; this bow tie is *prêt-à-porter*. With the addition of hair elastics or bobby pins, your new bow can even be used as a hair or shoe accessory! So go ahead — tie one (or two) on.

What You'll Need

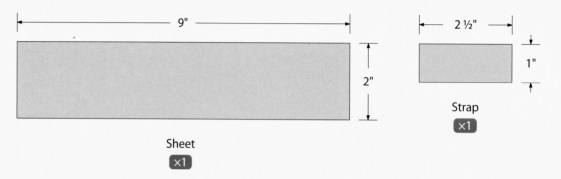

9"

2"

Sheet
×1

2 ½"

1"

Strap
×1

Make a 9" x 2" sheet from three pieces of tape folded over for the bow and a 2 ½" x 1" strap for the tie (see "How to Make Duct Tape Sheets" on page 8 and "How to Make Duct Tape Straps" on page 10).

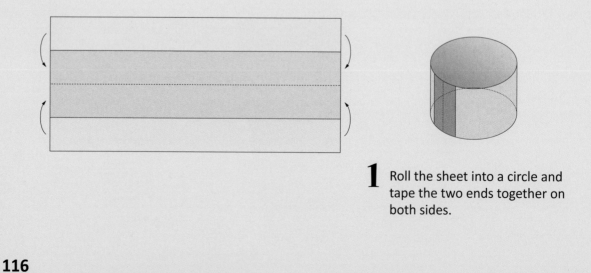

1 Roll the sheet into a circle and tape the two ends together on both sides.

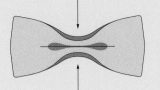

2 Flatten the circle with the seam in the middle underneath. At this stage, it's easier to decorate the bow before applying the tie, so have at it and add stripes, dots, squares of different colored duct tape. Pinch the flattened bow from the top and bottom to create a dent or recess in the middle along its front.

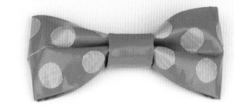

3 Take the strap and wrap it around the center of the bow where you have it pinched. Pulling it tightly around the bow, tape the strap ends together on both sides with a folded over piece of tape.

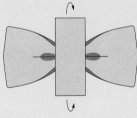

4 To don your new tie, make a thin strap that fits around your shirt collar and feed it behind the middle strap. Clip-ons are optional.

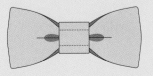

117

mad hatters

Walt Whitman once famously said, "I cock my hat as I please, indoors or out," and with these easy-to-make custom-fitted hats you too can brighten up Halloween, costume or office parties as either the Queen Mum or the Wicked Witch of the West! To make these hats you'll need to start with the size of your noggin (some math is required, parental discretion is advised, etc.). But once you get the hang of measuring and making the base, it's easy to create other headwear as deftly as an expert milliner. For example, made out of white or blue duct tape with gold stars, the cone of the witch's hat could double as a wizard's cap. Remove the rim from the leopard print hat and voilà — you have a pillbox hat.

What You'll Need

To determine the size of the sheets you will need, first measure the circumference of your head (B) using a sewing tape measure. Divide this by pi (3.14) for the diameter, rounding the number up if necessary (C). Add about 8" to this figure for the brim — this is the size of the square sheet you will need to make (A). Measure diagonally and mark the center point.

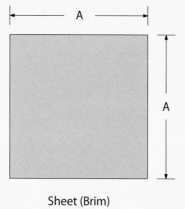

Sheet (Brim)
×1

B = Circumference of Head

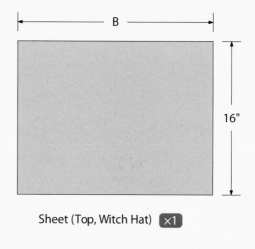

Sheet (Top, Witch Hat) ×1

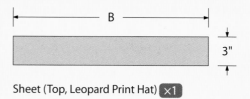

Sheet (Top, Leopard Print Hat) ×1

C = Diameter of Head (Diameter = Circumference / pi)

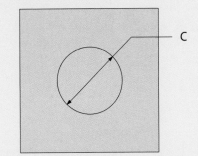

C

1 Take the diameter (C) you measured and divide it by two. Set a compass to this radius and, using the center point you marked, draw a circle of that diameter in the middle of the sheet.

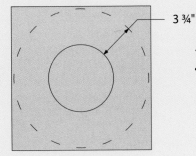

3 ¾"

2 Mark out a second circle with a radius 3 ¾" larger than the circle you drew in Step 1. To do this, use a ruler to mark 3 ¾" out from the edge of the first circle every couple of inches along its circumference. Draw the outer circle by connecting the marks.

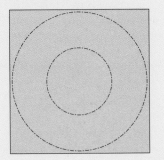

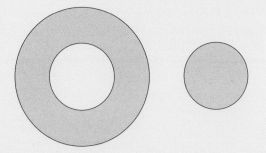

3 Cut out the inner circle you drew in Step 1 (If you are making the leopard print hat, keep this inner circle for later) and trim the outer circle you drew in Step 2. This is your hat's brim.

4 For the leopard print hat, first make a sheet that is 3" tall by the circumference of your head (B) (measured in What You'll Need). Wrap this sheet to make a circle, and tape the two ends together inside and out.

5 Tape the circle onto your brim inside and out, using 1" x 1" squares of tape (see "Taping Curved Edges" on page 12).

6 Take the inner circle you cut out in Step 3 and tape it to the top of your hat using the same technique as in Step 5.

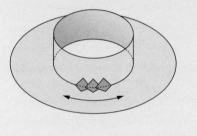

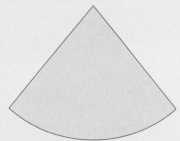

7 For the witch's hat, make a sheet 16" by the circumference of your head (B) (measured in What You'll Need). Mark the center of this sheet across the width of the top edge. From the center, measure 16" to one edge of the sheet and make a mark. Then make a series of 16" marks radially, from the center point every inch or so until you reach the other edge of the sheet. Connect the marks and cut out the resulting curve.

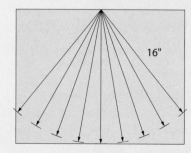

16"

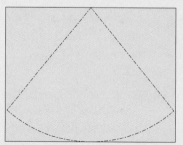

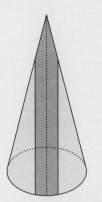

8 Fold the pie-shaped sheet around to create a cone, taping the two ends together inside and out.

9 Tape the cone to the brim you made in Steps 1 to 3, using the same taping technique as in Step 5. If you like, you can dress your sinister headgear up with a buckle or a spider or two.

123

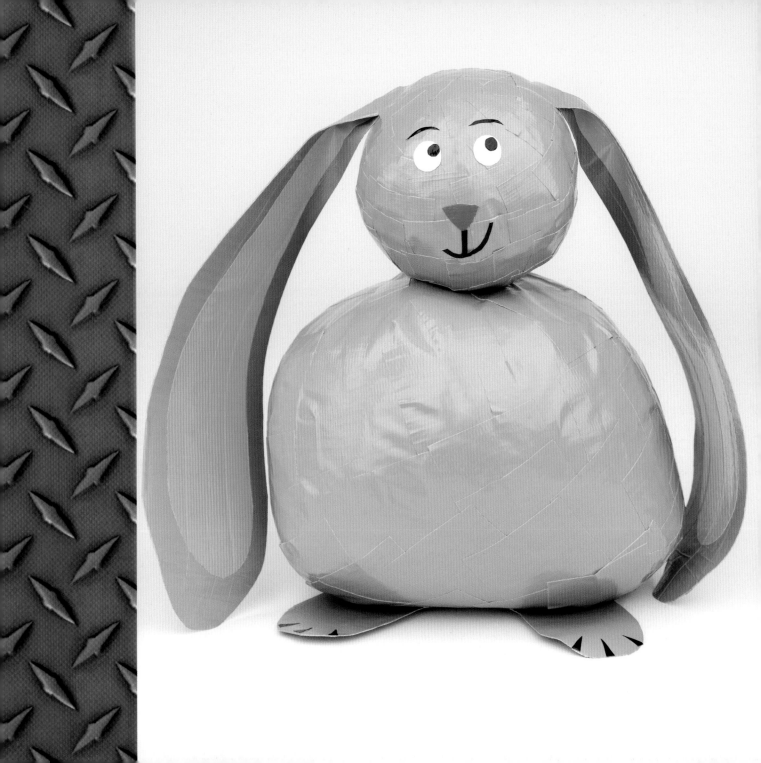

duct bunny

a sure sign of spring, rabbits are ancient symbols of fertility and Easter dating back to Anglo-Saxon times. (Female rabbits can conceive a second litter while pregnant with the first, so there's more than a little truth to the old adage "breed like rabbits.") Brought to North America by German immigrants in Pennsylvania during the 18th century, the "Osterhas" or Easter bunny quickly captured the imagination of children who believed that if they were good, a white rabbit would bring them gifts of brightly colored eggs in their caps and bonnets. In this project, Peter Cottontail gets a duct-tape makeover that's fun for the whole family to make.

What You'll Need

Make two sheets each for the ears and feet.

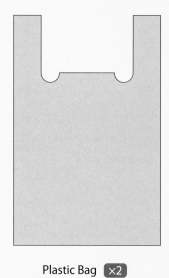

Plastic Bag ×2

11"

3"

Sheet (Ears) ×2

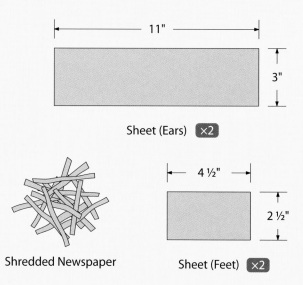

Shredded Newspaper

4 ½"

2 ½"

Sheet (Feet) ×2

1 Fill two plastic grocery bags with tightly packed shredded newspaper. Tie the bags with knots, pushing as much air out as you can. The bag for the body should be around 8" in diameter, the bag for the head about 4". Push the knots into the bag and tape them flat.

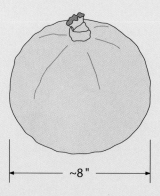

~8"

~4"

2 Cover the body and head with overlapping squares of duct tape (see "Taping Curved Surfaces" on page 13).

3 Tape the head onto the body at the back, using several overlapping rectangular pieces of tape. Push the tape as far as you can into the space between the head and body.

4 Draw and cut out the ears, around 2 ¾" at the widest part and 1" at the top. Fold the ears at the top and tape to the top of the head.

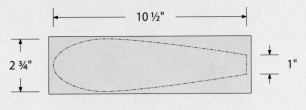

10 ½"

2 ¾"

1"

×2

4"

2"

1 ½"

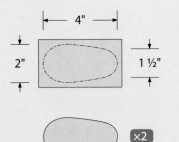

×2

5 Draw and cut out oblong shapes for the feet. Tape the feet to the underside of the body, leaving about 2" visible. Decorate your bunny's face, inside ears and toes!

basket case

a tisket, a tasket, duct tape woven basket! Made from strips of different colored tape woven together, this project uses the simplest form of weaving, plain weave, to create a pretty and colorful basket great for picking blueberries, carrying folders or folding laundry. Basket weaving beyond your skill set? It's actually not that difficult — if you ever watched your grandfather cane a chair or your mother lattice a pie, muttering "under over, under over" you'll pick up the technique. Once you've done one or two of different sizes you'll be hooked, and probably have a small cottage industry on your hands!

What You'll Need

To make the strips needed to weave the basket, tape two pieces of duct tape together, sticky sides facing each other, then cut in half lengthwise. This will give you two strips. You will need 12 strips that are 26" long, 8 that are 30" long and 7 that are 40" long. (If you want your basket to have a checkered pattern, the 40" strips should be a different color than the other two.) Make your strips at least 2" longer than required so you don't have to line them all up perfectly even (the strips will shift as you weave). If you find the length of the strips too difficult to work with, you can cut strips half the length and tape them together (see "Taping Flat Surfaces" on page 11).

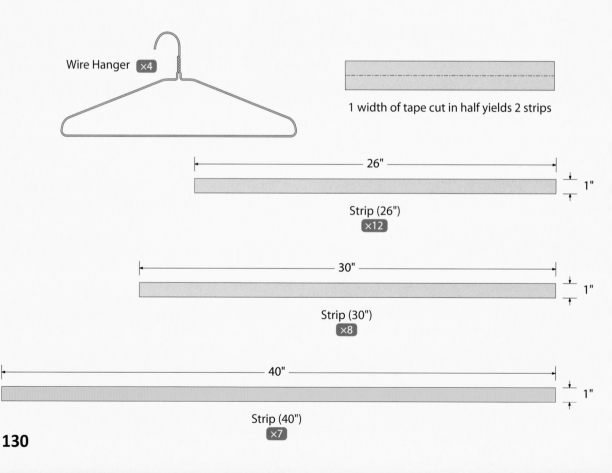

Wire Hanger ×4

1 width of tape cut in half yields 2 strips

26"   1"

Strip (26")
×12

30"   1"

Strip (30")
×8

40"   1"

Strip (40")
×7

1 To make the base of the basket, lay the 26" strips flat and weave the 30" strips into them, alternating over one, under one, creating a rectangle in the center as tightly woven as possible. You can tape the edges of the woven base to keep the strips from moving. (If you do, use masking tape because, unlike duct tape, it's easy to remove later!).

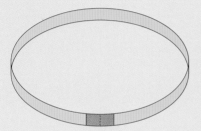

2 Next tape the ends of each 40" strip together to make seven large loops. These will be woven into the sides of the basket.

3 Start weaving the loose ends of the basket base through the 40" loops from Step 2, alternating over one, under one. Slide the first circle down to the base. Weave the second loop, offsetting the pattern by one square, and repeat with the remaining loops, keeping them tightly stacked one atop the other. After a few have been woven in, the basket shape will start to form and be easier to hold together.

4 Take two of the four wire coat hangers and use wire cutters to cut the hooks off. Cut and bend what remains to form a U-shape that measures 12" x 8". Repeat with the second coat hanger and place the two together to form a rectangle as shown. Wrap with tape. Repeat with the other two coat hangers.

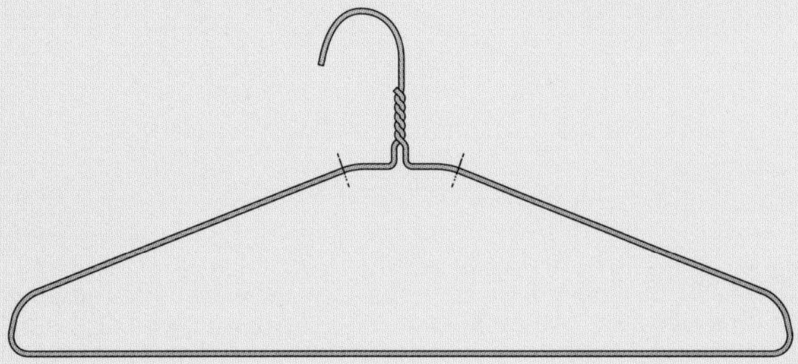

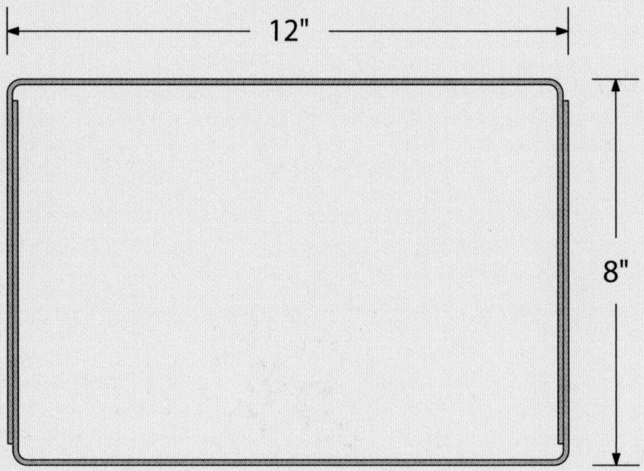

12"

8"

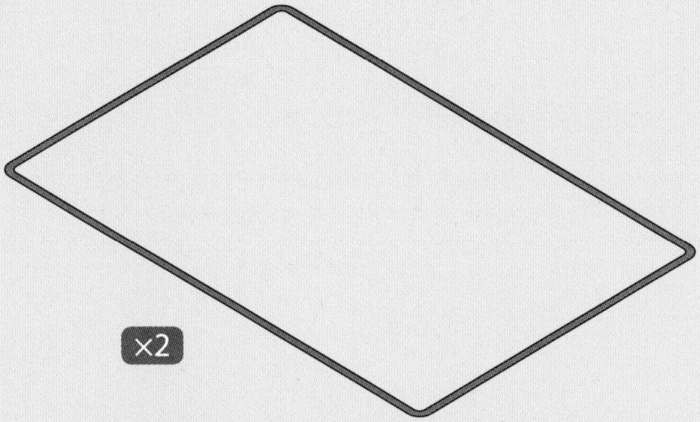

×2

5 Wrap the ends of the woven basket strips around one of the rectangles you made in Step 4, alternating over one, under one. Trim the ends of the strips; they should be no longer than ¾" to 1", just enough to tape them down in place.

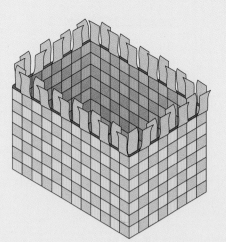

6 Seal all four edges of the basket with strips of tape.

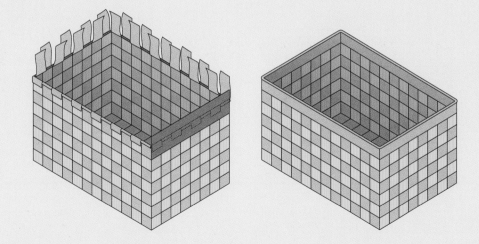

7 Place the second rectangle you made in Step 4 at the base of the basket for support.

analog photo album

the trusty photo album is a foolproof gift, for it's a clean slate to be filled by the recipient and it sends the message that we really do want them to record our memories for posterity and have our crossed eyes immortalized between covers for the ages. First made by scientists to record photographic experiments, photo albums quickly went from being fuddy old leather-bound research journals to gilded, inlaid and bejeweled collections of family snapshots upon the advent of professional photo studios in the late 1850s. Sure, you can upload a million JPEGs to Flickr but where's the personal touch in that? What if Grandma doesn't have a wireless hotspot? Duct tape to the rescue! Save your photographic keepsakes — summer vacation, baby's first steps, weddings, parties, anything — in this decidedly analog album.

What You'll Need

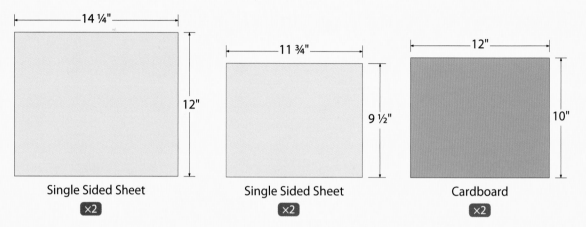

14 ¼"

12"

Single Sided Sheet
×2

11 ¾"

9 ½"

Single Sided Sheet
×2

12"

10"

Cardboard
×2

Cut out two 12" x 10" pieces of cardboard and make four single-sided (one side sticky) sheets, two measuring 11 ¾" x 9 ½" and two measuring 14 ¼" x 12".

1 For the spine, cut 1" off the end of both pieces of cardboard as shown.

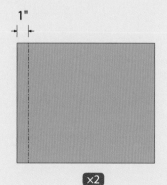

1"

×2

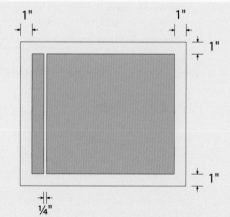

1" 1" 1" ¼" 1"

2 Lie one of the 14 ¼" x 12" sheets flat, sticky side up. On the left side of the sheet, carefully place one of the 1" strips of cardboard about 1" in from the left side and 1" from the top and bottom. Leaving a small ¼" gap, place one of the larger pieces of cardboard to the right of the strip.

3 Cut the four corners of the sheet at a 45° angle, so the corners of the cardboard are at the edge of the cuts. Fold each edge of the sheet over onto the cardboard.

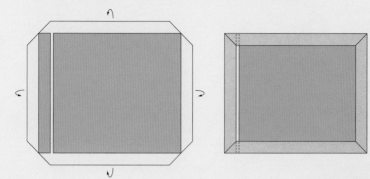

4 Place one of the 9 ½" x 11 ¾" sheets sticky side down in the center, covering the exposed cardboard. Leave a ¼" border all around. Repeat Steps 2 to 4 for the back cover of the album.

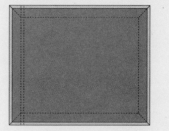

5 Stack the two album covers and secure them together with fold-back clips or tape. Make three holes in the spine ½" in from the left edge, one in the center (5" down) and two about 1" from the top and bottom. Decorate the cover and tie together with string or ribbon.

The Cover Up

Once you have some experience under your belt creating projects and have an honorary Doctorate of Ductology, put your home taping skills to good use and breathe some new life into old objects. Spruce up a pair of drab sneakers with zippy new colors, fashion funky striped gift boxes out of cardboard lying around the house, cover an old book or a new e-reader, revive a cast-off picture frame with floral decorations (see page 25), or go big and re-cover a favorite chair (We know what you're thinking — but have you priced reupholstering a wing chair recently?) It's so easy there's no step-by-step! Just remember your basics, use colored and/or patterned duct tape (here we redid our chair in a chevron theme using a zig zag pattern), overlap your strips and finish any edges and ends. You've heard the phrase "nothing that a lick of paint won't fix?" Well, substitute "a strip of tape" and you too can achieve stunning results and stylish design on a dime.

passport pal

around 450 BC, Nehemiah, an aid in the employ of King Artaxerxes I of Persia, wished to travel to Judea, and to ensure his safe passage the king sent him with a letter requesting that he pass freely without delay or hindrance. Now, this being over 2,400 years ago, Nehemiah really had nothing to carry his newfangled "passport" in, but if he'd had a few rolls of the tape he could have whipped up this nifty one with pockets for traveling plastic, papers and coin, all exquisitely tooled and individually designed. Since we are asked to produce our passports when traveling more times than Nehemiah would have ever imagined, we might as well look good doing it. So whether you make it funky or elegant, protect your passport in nothing less.

What You'll Need

Make a 7 ½" x 5 ¼" inside sheet and an 8" x 5 ¼" outside sheet.

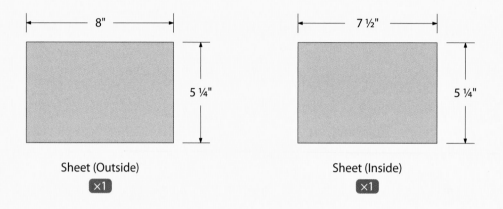

Sheet (Outside)
×1

Sheet (Inside)
×1

1 Cut the inside sheet in half vertically. Take the right half and seal its left edge with a ½" wide piece of tape.

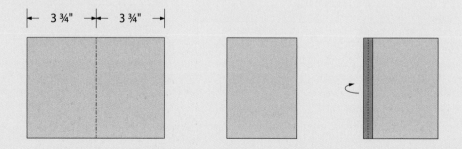

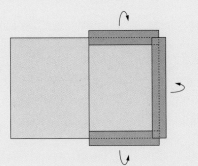

2 Lay the right half of the inside sheet atop the outside sheet on the right side, aligning the outside edges, and seal them with tape. Don't tape the inner (left) edge that you taped in Step 1.

3 To make the wallet pockets, take two 3 ¾" long pieces of tape and stick the sticky sides together, overlapping them so that ¼" of the sticky surface is exposed at the top and bottom. Fold over both edges to seal. Repeat six times.

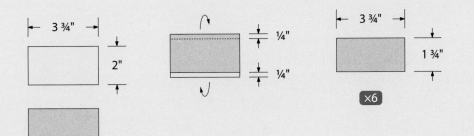

4 Space out the pockets evenly on the left half of the inside sheet from Step 1, placing the top folded seams of the pockets face down so they are not visible. Secure the pockets to the sheet with tape along both sides of their bottom edges. Tape the bottom pocket to the sheet on the inside only.

5 Secure the right side of the pockets to the sheet with a ¾" wide piece of tape, folding it around to the back of the sheet. Carefully cut the folded tape along the tops of the pockets to reopen them.

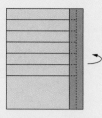

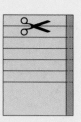

6 Lay the pocket assembly atop the left side of the outside sheet assembly from Step 2. Seal the outer edges with ¾" wide pieces of tape. Reopen the pockets on the left side as in Step 5.

7 Flip the wallet over and reinforce the center spine with tape. Decorate!

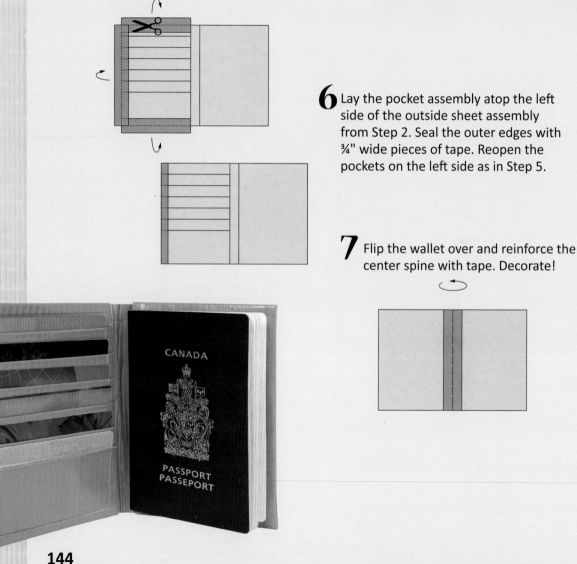